Always Ride the Carousel

A Child's Cancer Diagnosis, A Parent's Journey

By

Philip D. Weber

Special thanks to Rachel Weber and Meaghan Miller for the cover photographs and Jill Kjorlien for the illustration.

This book is a work of non-fiction. All of the names used herein are used with permission and where permission could not be secured, for whatever reason, the names were omitted. All opinions and observations are those of the author of this work.

ISBN 10 1533467331
ISBN 13 978-1533467331

First paperback edition: July, 2016

Table of Contents

Dedication

No one should have to go through cancer alone. We were lucky. We had a huge team that supported us during our journey. Our families were amazing and our friends beyond amazing. I've heard that the best test of a friendship is to need someone. We needed them and they passed the test with flying colors. Some were willing to put their own health at risk as potential living organ donors. Others planned events and took care of dozens of details which we would have overlooked during those manic days. Still others offered invaluable encouragement through their thoughts, prayers, and positive energy. We wouldn't have made it through that time without their help.

My students, Weber's Warriors, never let me down. They stepped up in ways we couldn't have expected. Their empathy and thoughtfulness were amazing and they made me proud to know them.

Our medical teams were fantastic. Our doctors became friends and our nurses became family. I don't know how they do those jobs day in and day out. It is clearly not just a job, but a calling.

To all of these people I offer my sincere thanks. In their own ways each of them lit a candle for us during our darkest hours.

I want to thank Jill Kjorlien, the cover artist. She was a great friend as we were going through David's diagnosis and treatment. Today, she remains a great friend, and a great artist.

I have to acknowledge August Cassens and Caitlin Perry, the associate editors for this project. These young women worked at my old college newspaper. I didn't want to turn it over to the actual editors and publishers without having another set of eyes to look things over and make me look good. I told them I could pay them in "beer money, not rent money" but they believed the story was worth telling. They had great ideas and really boosted my confidence. Several friends also volunteered to give the final draft a once-over and provided some invaluble advice.

All of these people earned their carousel tokens.

This book, however, is dedicated to those parents and families that are just starting their own journeys. There will be dark, dark days ahead but I want them to remember that the light still exists even when they can't see it.

Fight hard against those moments when hope seems far away and do not let yourselves be overwhelmed with despair.

Laugh when you can.

Cry when you have to.

Never apologize for how you feel and always ride the carousel.

PW

Foreword

By

Dr. Sharon McDonald
St. Louis Children's Hospital

Many parts of my job have become routine over time: the
writing of chemotherapy, procedures including bone marrow
aspirations and lumbar punctures, and other day-to-day tasks that
make up the life of a pediatric hematologist-oncologist. The one part
that never becomes routine is delivering bad news to families –
whether that is their initial diagnosis or offering hospice after all else
has failed.

No matter what your socioeconomic, racial, religious, or
educational status is, being told your child has cancer has the same
effect on a parent. You develop a sense of hopelessness. In most
cases, I can assuage this fear with reminders to families that the
treatment of childhood cancer has improved dramatically over the
past half century. For instance, the survival rate for one of the most
common childhood cancers, acute lymphoblastic leukemia, is now
more than 80 percent which has come a long way from the 1950's
when it was uniformly fatal. However, these are still rare pediatric
cancers that have associated poor prognoses, and research is
occurring at several levels to help improve these outcomes.

I met the Weber family, as usual, under the worst of

circumstances – when David was first diagnosed with a tumor in his liver. Unfortunately, his particular tumor was quite rare and, as such, had a poor prognosis despite chemotherapy, surgery, and radiation. In spite of delivering all of this news and relaying the hard months that were ahead for David, his parents displayed a strength and compassion for their child and each other that I marveled at.

So many times, the stress of having a child with cancer is too overwhelming for many families, and instead of finding strength in each other, I see marriages and families crumble under the struggle.

For David, his road would include intensive chemotherapy according to a new protocol that was aimed at treatment of his particularly rare case followed by a liver transplant to allow the tumor to be fully resected. Throughout his treatment, his parents displayed courage and an ability to see beyond the cancer that I wished other families of mine could have. And after the chemotherapy failed, and David progressed with metastatic disease, his parents amazed me further by asking whether David could donate his tumor to science because they wanted his life, as short as it was, to have as much impact as possible. I didn't say it at the time, but David had an enormous impact on my life as well as the lives of nurses and other doctors at the hospital – as well his parents – with their amazing coping strategies and strength.

During the discussion about end of life care for David, Phil mentioned in passing that he might write a book for parents of newly diagnosed children with cancer. I can't recall what I relayed to him, but I remember thinking that if there was any way he could somehow give their gift of compassion, coping skills, and strength to other families, it would be wonderful. When I received the request for the interview not long after David had passed away, I was astounded. In the short time I had known the Webers, they had never ceased to amaze me.

If by reading this you can take away even a quarter of the amazing qualities that these parents have, then I believe you will do well. And with that, David will have lived on and touched even more lives.

Introduction

First let me say, please do not look at this book as a "How To" book on dealing with a child's cancer. There are plenty of other books out there written by people who are vastly more intelligent than I am to which you can turn for "How To" help. In fact, many of the passages here could probably be seen as a "How Not To" guide of things to avoid.

Those of us confronting cancer share many thoughts, fears, feelings, worries, and events , but each story (like each child) is unique. This is my personal story and, right or wrong, this is the way I dealt with this journey.

The first part of this book was originally written as a journal of my experiences. As we received early information about our son, we had crazy thoughts about how to pass on this information to friends, family, coworkers, etc. without offending anyone who didn't make the "personal phone call" list. This is the kind of thing we worry about when we first get a diagnosis and haven't yet learned how to put ourselves first. One of the nurses suggested I start a blog to keep everyone informed. It was a Godsend, as I could put in the information once and then walk away. Before long the information-only blog turned into an on-line diary of sorts. I started writing about how I felt and allowed myself to be completely honest and vulnerable in ways I couldn't have been if I'd been giving information out face-to-face or over the phone.

Eventually people started sharing my blog with others in

similar situations. I found myself connecting with people around the world that I'd never met, people who said that seeing somone else going through the same frustrations and fears somehow made them feel better. I have to agree, and that is my hope in sharing this with you now.

Be forewarned that this is not a feel-good inspirational story. It doesn't end well. In writing this book I've tried to be as honest as I could. I was often writing moments after learning some new information, so my writing was often raw and real and emotional. I'm sure I've made mistakes, or contradicted myself, especially with some of the medical details because memories can be a bit jumbled at times like those.

The first part of this book was originally written as a journal of my experiences. I was often writing only moments after learning some new information. It is possible, even likely, that some of the information here is incorrect and sometimes even contradicts itself. Again, the only excuse I have is that I'm not a doctor and this was a dizzying emotional time. I apologize if things are confusing from time to time.

Confusion is part of the journey.

The second part of this book is something that comes close to a "How To" style. I put my journalism cap back on and interviewed several doctors, social workers, and others, including some of the leading experts in their fields, so I could include information that could be helpful to other parents in similar situations.

In addition to my story, and to help others lessen some of their confusion, I wanted to include information that might be useful to other parents, family members, and friends who find themselves in similar situations. So I spoke to several doctors, social workers, nurses, and others, including some of the leading experts in their fields.

Let me end this introduction at the beginning: the "before," so to speak. My wife, Rachel, and I purposely waited to have children until we were certain we were mature enough and stable enough in our relationship to handle anything that parenthood threw at us.

Boy, were we ever wrong about that assumption.

David was born on June 15, 2007, almost a month premature but otherwise a perfect, healthy baby boy. He had a healthy birth weight and strong lungs. He was a little jaundiced, which is common for premature babies, but we were released from the hospital after only a few days. I can remember driving him home that first day and thinking something along the lines of, "Whew! The worst is over. Every kid spends a little time in the hospital while they are growing up. David just got his out of the way early. He's going to be perfectly healthy from now on."

I was wrong about that assumption too.

David was six months old when his problems began.

Part I

"Some of the most comforting words in the universe are, 'me too.' That moment when you find out that your struggle is also someone else's struggle, that you are not alone, and that others have been down that same road."

– Author unknown

This was the first e-mail I sent to my sister about David. At the time, we didn't know how serious his situation was. We soon learned.

Jan. 9, 2008, 7:31 a.m.

I've got some bad news to share, and I don't have time to make a phone call. We took David to the doctor the other day because he's been sick for a while – seemed like he had a mild case of the flu but it was holding on too long. They took some blood and had an ultrasound. They found spots on his liver and his liver is enlarged. We're going in this afternoon to talk with the doctor, so we'll know more then. I'll try to let you know as soon as we hear anything.

Hope for the best!

This was a mass e-mail to most of our friends, family members, co-workers, and a few of my students' parents. This was the first time most of them learned anything was wrong.

Jan. 11, 2008, 4:30 p.m.

Hey everybody, sorry for the mass e-mail but things have been kind of hectic around here lately. I'm also sorry if this is repeated information for anybody. I haven't slept much lately so I don't really remember who I've talked to and who I haven't. Forgive me if I ramble.

David has liver cancer. We have caught it very early and the doctors think the prognosis is very good. We are staying at St. Louis Children's Hospital, the No. 6 hospital in the country and our doctor is one who – LITERALLY – writes the book on liver re-growth after injury and illness. This is his main focus for the past ten years. We're confident that we can and will beat this thing.

The team of oncologists, transplant specialists, etc. are meeting with us today. We are almost certainly going to have a biopsy this afternoon so the team can find out what kind of cancer we're looking at and how we should treat it. The tests so far have shown that the cancer is within the liver, not around the liver. This is a good thing because the cancer is much less likely to spread to other systems if it is contained within one organ.

The doctors conducted a CAT scan yesterday. They said most of the right lobe (the big one) of the liver has been corrupted. The cancer has also invaded the left lobe (the little one), but not as much. Our doctor (the guy who writes the book) said we only need 25 percent of our livers to be healthy to re-grow the rest of it (who knew?). He said he thought about 60 percent of David's liver overall has been corrupted, so that leaves him plenty left to work with if doctors have to remove the damaged material.

We'll know more once other tests come back. We may be in line for a transplant, but it is way too early to say anything like that. The good news about transplants (from a donor point-of-view) is that donated material grows back and, because he's so little, doctors wouldn't have to take much from the donor. The line to become a donor forms behind me, if it comes to that.

Worst case scenario (other than something completely unexpected) is that he's sick for a little while, has some surgery, and then goes on to lead a normal life. The doctors say there is a "high probability of successful outcome" with any of the types of cancer this could likely be.

Our spirits are pretty high. Lack of sleep is taking its toll, but other than that we are all doing well. David is still happy and, seemingly, healthy. He doesn't act like a sick baby. He laughs and plays and takes naps. The only time his spirits are low is when they tell us that we can't feed him because of some upcoming test. I know it sounds corny, but he is an inspiration and I'm proud of him. He has a lot of his great-grandfather in him and people who knew Don Schopp know that's a good thing. Rachel and I are holding up pretty well too. We have a few bad moments, but they are rare, and we work through them together.

I expect that we'll be down here in St. Louis for quite a while, but I really don't know. It is possible that we'll be home early next week (I hope). I'll try to send other e-mails to update everybody if I learn anything new.

Thanks everyone for all of the support and prayers. We have

the best friends and families we could ever ask for. Everyone has rallied around us, and we love you for it.

Jan. 13, 2008, 10:22 a.m.

David is scheduled for a biopsy tomorrow morning so the doctors can find out exactly what type of cancer they are dealing with. Once they know that they will know what kind of chemotherapy will work best against it. Doctors will also install a semi-permanent IV tube in David's chest. The tube will make it a lot easier for them to give him the chemo, take blood, start IVs, etc. With this tube in place, they won't have to stick him in the arm every time they need something. It will save him a lot of pain.
David's spirits are high even though he wants to go home and sleep in his own bed. We can tell that he misses seeing the kids at Dena's (his daycare provider - great lady) because every time he sees a child in the hall his eyes lock on them and he won't pay attention to anything else.

We have been receiving amazing support from friends and family. Everyone we know has gone way beyond anything we could have hoped for.

Jan. 14, 2008, 9:09 a.m.

David went in for the biopsy at about 7:45 a.m. today, a bit earlier than we expected. That was a happy surprise because now we won't have to wait as long for results. So what if it meant that I had to run to the operating room without socks and Rachel had wet hair.

We expect that this tumor will be an embryonic sarcoma – a type of cancer he's been growing since conception.

The doctors will keep David under anesthetic until the earliest results of the biopsy come back. If it is the type of cancer they expect, they will have to install a tube in his chest for drawing blood, injecting chemo, etc. He will stay out so that they won't have to anesthetize him a second time.

Jan. 14, 2008, 11:15 a.m.

David is out of surgery. Everything went well. He is a little sore on his stomach, but otherwise he isn't too bad. He even managed to smile at me a bit, so I take that as a good sign – of course, that could have been the morphine

David's surgeon said it is almost certainly a malignant cancer, but he couldn't be certain about which kind of cancer it is until the test results come back. Now it is a bit of a waiting game. The results could be here as early as sometime this afternoon or it could take as long as two days for them to come back.

Rachel and I are both relieved that David seems to be comfortable and there were no complications. David is relieved that he finally gets to eat again. He hadn't eaten since 2 a.m. Now he can have some water or juice and soon he will be back on his regular formula.

We've had a lot of kind messages. I know it sounds cheesy, but it really makes Rachel and I feel so much better to know we have this kind of support. I especially like hearing from current and former students (sorry adults, but that's how it is).

Jan. 14, 2008, 1:57 p.m.

Things are still going well. David is a bit groggy, but he wakes up for brief periods from time-to-time. He has started drinking already. We have some good news too. David will be staying on the eighth floor at SLCH.

This is good for two reasons: First, the nurses on the floor love him and take turns trying to spoil him. Second, it means his immune system is strong enough to be around other patients. If his immune system was a bit weaker, the doctors would have moved him to the special "clean" rooms of the ninth floor. It is possible that we will move to the ninth floor sometime soon, but that is only because that's where the chemo treatments and the oncology specialists are located. For now, eighth floor is a good thing.

Jan. 14, 2008, 5:19 p.m.

Well, our stay on the eighth floor is a bit of a mixed blessing. Yes, we wanted to be there because it means his immune system is still strong enough to be around other kids. The downside, however, is that now we have a roommate. She's a sweet little girl who is also seven months old. The nurses said she sleeps through the night and almost never cries. All week the nurses on the floor have said that the girl, Faith, is going to be David's girlfriend and now they've got the two of them "shackin' up together." Hehehe.

We just spoke to the doctors and there really isn't any news.

The biopsy results will not be in until tomorrow. That's about what we expected, but not quite what we'd hoped. The surgeon said he couldn't see anything that resembled a normal liver but qualified that statement by saying he only had about a three-quarter inch hole to look through. We are still almost certain that a transplant will be needed.

I managed to get a legitimate, albeit small, giggle out of David a little bit ago. He is in a little pain when he moves, but he seems happy enough when he's sitting still.

Jan. 15, 2008, 7:20 p.m.

Well, we're still not sure what the cancer is or when we'll be coming home. The doctors have narrowed it down to two possible types - both of which have long medical names that don't mean anything to me. The pathology folks are doing a series of stains - which also doesn't mean much to me - that should tell them exactly what we're looking at. They probably won't have the results until later this week.

We had thought we might be able to come home Wednesday afternoon and return to St. Louis to begin the treatments whenever the doctors settled on what to do. However, there might be a wrinkle there. The doctors told us this evening that they want to do a bone marrow test to be certain that the cancer hasn't spread. They'll let us know Wednesday morning when they can schedule that procedure, which means our plans for returning home might be delayed.

I'll talk with the doctors more tomorrow for more information but as far as I know the bone marrow thing involves putting David under general anesthesia and inserting a needle into the bones of his hip to remove a bit of bone marrow. I don't know how painful this is going to be but I can't imagine it's going to be pleasant.

Still, Rachel and I are taking positive steps. I learned from one of the doctors that I am probably blood type O, the same as David. That means I am a good candidate as a potential liver donor. I'm getting tested tomorrow morning, beginning with a psychological exam which somehow worries me more than the physical stuff.

Rachel took a positive step of her own today. She had most of her hair cut off and donated it to Locks of Love. For anyone who doesn't know, that is an organization that takes donated hair and makes wigs for chemo patients who have lost their hair because of the treatments. I think Rachel looks amazing with short hair, which is a good thing because her hair is now almost as short as mine. WOW!

We also had some good news on a financial issue we were worried about. The overall cost of the transplant is going to be something in the neighborhood of $425,000. Ugh! We talked to the financial consultant about all of those issues and she said she has already talked with the insurance company and most of this is going to be covered (once again, thank God for Rachel's employers and their commitment to their employees in getting good insurance). The consultant also showed us several ways to make the remaining costs considerably less of a burden.

In another bit of good news David is acting like his old self today. He's laughing, sitting up, rolling over and generally behaving like a happy baby who doesn't have any pain. The only thing that bothers him is that we won't let him chew on the tube running from his chest to the IV unit by the bed. He is eating well and generally enjoying the attention from all of the nurses, most of whom are spoiling him.

Thanks everyone for the prayers and positive energy that keeps heading our way. Somehow saying "thank you" doesn't seem good enough. We are unbelievably fortunate to have the support and love of friends and family. We couldn't do this without them.

Jan. 16, 2008, 5:49 p.m.

We received bad news today. Doctors have identified David's cancer as a rhabdoid sarcoma. This is a very rare cancer, so rare that there are fewer than fifty cases ever begun in a patient's liver.

Doctors said there are two types of rhabdoid sarcoma. The first (which we are hoping for) stays in the liver and can be treated with chemotherapy and a liver transplant. This is more serious than what we originally thought but the doctors said there is a good chance that he will be fine. They said it is better than 50/50 but they wouldn't say how much better. Dr. Shepherd would only say that there is a "reasonably good chance" of a positive outcome.

The second type of rhabdoid sarcoma is aggressive and devastating. It is a pervasive genetic mutation that could replicate itself throughout David's body. Once this spreads out to other organs there is very little chance of surviving. As far as we know only one person has ever survived with this second type of rhabdoid sarcoma.

If David has this type of cancer, the doctors will treat it with chemotherapy but they won't give him a liver transplant because it probably wouldn't be enough to really help.

The doctors don't think David has this second type of cancer, but they have to admit that it is a possibility. They have already checked all of his organs, his skin, his blood and, as of this afternoon, his bone and bone marrow. They didn't find any trace of the cancer in these places. We are setting up for an MRI either Thursday or Friday to check out David's brain.

The doctors believe it is a very good sign that they haven't seen the cancer anywhere else and they don't expect to find it in his brain.

We do have some positive steps to take. Many people have said they are interested in becoming living liver donors. In order to be considered as a potential donor someone must be at least 18 years old, be in reasonably good physical condition, have their own health insurance and have the correct blood type. Our insurance covers all of the donor's expenses for the surgery and recovery but the donor has to have their own insurance in case of complications years down the road.

Jan. 17, 2008, 9:28 a.m.

We're scheduled for an MRI sometime Friday morning. Once that is finished we will have a better idea of what type of rhabdoid sarcoma we're dealing with. If we find cancer in David's brain, we'll know we're dealing with the more aggressive genetic mutation type.

That would be very bad. If we don't find cancer in his brain we still have to wait a few weeks for the genetic tests to come back to be certain one way or the other.

David will have a localized ultrasound on his liver today to see how his blood vessels are holding up. This test should be sometime this morning. The sooner the better because David hasn't eaten since about 4 a.m. to prepare for the test. We did a similar ultrasound in Champaign, but I understand why the doctors in St. Louis want to do their own tests. Not only are they probably wary of results that they didn't come up with themselves, but it's been a week since the first ultrasound and things might have changed.

David is still laughing, smiling and playing just like always. Seeing him in action renews my faith that things will be okay.

Jan. 17, 2008, 5:20 p.m.

We're celebrating a little bit tonight ... or should I say a little bite tonight? David's first tooth came through today. The first of many to come.

Jan. 18, 2008, 10:34 a.m.

David just left for an MRI. Doctors are checking to see if the cancer has spread to his brain. We don't expect that it has but we need to be sure.

He was flirting with the nurses as they took him away so I'm fairly sure he isn't scared. Last time they took him for a test like this he came back stoned out of his mind. The drugs they give him to

calm him down are apparently quite strong and can cause mild hallucinations. The nurses last time told us that older children have reported seeing flowers and colors. Rarely, some children have also reported seeing things that are not-so-friendly, like spiders and other bugs. Eeewwww!

David will get his first round of chemotherapy tonight. We hope things go well and that his white blood count doesn't drop too low. He has to have a certain level (I have no idea how much) of white blood cells before he is allowed to go back to his daycare. He really misses daycare and his friends so we are praying that he gets to go.

We are expecting to come home within a few days. If his white blood count is strong enough we'll try bringing him around to visit people. Of course, this all depends on the results of this MRI today. If they find cancer in his brain everything changes.

Jan. 18, 2008, 6:11 p.m.

David's MRI came back with the news we wanted to hear. The cancer did not spread to his brain. This doesn't mean that the tumor in his liver isn't the more aggressive genetic problem that we're worried about, but it gives us hope for when the final tests come back in a few weeks.

We started the chemotherapy a few minutes ago. We're hoping the medicine he took to keep him feeling good will be strong enough to counteract the chemicals in the chemo that could make him feel bad. I'd give you some names but there is a whole pharmacy of

things they are pumping into him so I'm sure I'd get some of them wrong.

The worst effect tonight will probably be that David feels very sick to his stomach and that he fills his diaper way more often than usual. The other bad effect is that one of the drugs – the one nicknamed "The Red Devil" and "Ruby Red" – will likely turn his fluids red. His urine and his tears will both be red. I'm glad they warned me ahead of time, or that would have been a really big shock.

David will almost certainly have to have a blood transfusion tonight. His red cell count is low, but only just a little. On a scale of 1-10 (10 being the best) David was at a 7.5. Doctors recommend blood transfusions for anything less than 8. I'm not sure exactly why his cell count dropped, but the doctors said it could be as simple as the fact that they've drawn a lot of blood in the last few days for tests.

Our return home may be delayed by a day because of the transfusion and some odd timing/scheduling problems. If David's white blood count is strong enough we'll try to bring him around to see people. The visits may be fairly short as Rachel and I are both very tired and David might still be feeling the effects of the chemo.

We'll see how David handles the chemo tonight. That should give us a good idea of how the next few months are going to go.

We got some good news today. It seems that there is a pediatric oncologist (cancer specialist) in Champaign that can give David some of his chemo treatments. This means we won't have to spend

so much time on the road and in St. Louis.

On the lighter side (well, lighter now that I've calmed down) one of the nurses in our room took her life in her hands with an offhand comment. She saw that I was feeling a little frustrated and she made a quip about how the comic shop I visited earlier today must not have had the books I wanted.

Don't tease a frustrated nerd about his comics. That's like poking a grizzly bear in the eye with a stick and expecting it to just walk away without mauling you (OK that analogy is a bit too strong, but you get the idea).

After gritting my teeth and, as calmly as possible, explaining that it really wasn't the best time to joke with me, she got the hint and quickly left the room. Now that I have a little distance from the situation I can see how silly it was and that she was just doing what I normally do - make a stupid joke to try to ease the tension. The situation did have a positive ending though.

I found out that Dr. McDonald, David's main doctor, was also a comic-book geek and loved Joss Whedon, the nerd icon who gave us *Firefly*, one of the best sci-fi series ever brought to television. [Although I didn't have any way of knowing at the time, Whedon would go on to write and direct *The Avengers* and *Avengers: Age of Ultron* – two of the biggest movies ever. Maybe you've heard of them?] We talked a bit and I quickly relaxed. All I needed was to talk to "my people" for a while.

She even understood when I complained that the comic shop seemed too clean to be a "real comic shop." There were no month-old pizza boxes lying around. There were no teetering stacks of comics waiting to be sorted. There were no fat bearded guys who hadn't washed since the Clinton administration sitting in the corner arguing about which team is better The Avengers or the JLA (by the way, the JLA kicks Avenger butt).

It didn't feel like home and Dr. McDonald understood what I meant. I like her.

Jan. 19, 2008, 10:04 a.m.

Last night was probably the hardest night of my life and, if the nurses are correct, tonight could be just as bad. David started chemotherapy yesterday and he was inconsolable by evening. The "uncomfortable" feeling that the nurses had described was in full effect - and then some. We spent a lot of time pacing around the halls and our room. It was very tense for a few hours but we got through it.

David finally slept at about 4 a.m. today, but he was grinning again when he woke up this morning at about 8:30 a.m. and we couldn't help but grin right back at him. We take that as a good sign.

The nurses said he will likely be very sleepy today and tonight so it is possible that he will sleep through the worst of the "discomfort." We hope so.

I feel like I've been awake for weeks (come to think of it, I almost have). Our friends keep sending us their thoughts, prayers, and positive energy. God bless them for caring. We'll get through this.

Jan. 19, 2008, 7:41 p.m.

So far, so good. Today has been a very good day for David. He played quite a bit. He got to ride around the hospital in a wagon, grinning like a king looking out on his adoring subjects. He spent quite a bit of time inside a "pillow fort" we made for him so he could sit up on his own for longer periods of time without us worrying that he was going to break his neck if he fell over.

Most importantly, he got to sleep a bit more today than other days. Oh what a glorious feeling it is to have a sleeping baby at times like these. Whew. It probably did Rachel and I more good to have that quiet time than it did for him.

He just finished his second batch of the two-day cycle of chemo. This is a smaller group of medicine (more "Red Devil" though) so we're hoping he won't be in as much discomfort tonight. So far he's still feeling good. We'll know more in a few hours. He's been eating fairly well tonight which means that the nausea associated with the chemo hasn't hit him too hard. Now we know, though, that we shouldn't wait for him to become completely freaked out.

If it looks like he is in a lot of pain (kind of like last night) we should ask the nurses for his pain medication right away. We know what the warning signs are now (I think) so it shouldn't get that far anymore. We'll be bringing some of that medication home with us too so we can handle things there if we have to.

The nurses offered to take David for a little while this

afternoon so Rachel and I could go outside the hospital for lunch. We walked over to a nearby restaurant and felt completely normal for a change. We stopped feeling like patients and started feeling like people. I guess it was a good day for all three of us.

Jan. 20, 2008, 10:25 a.m.

Last night was one of our best since we've been here. The nurses must have been trained by ninjas. We didn't hear them all night, yet they still managed to come in to take David's vital signs, change his diapers, and do all the other things they do without waking us up. All three of us managed to get quite a bit of good sleep last night - something we all really needed.

It was also a good night for David. He had a bit of pain mid-evening, but the medications took care of that. He has also developed a raging case of chemo rash. That's like diaper rash only it is caused by the chemicals in his urine from the chemotherapy. He went from a perfectly normal little tushie to a bright red (think bad sunburn) tushie in only a few hours. The nurses were expecting this, and they worked up some kind of a cream that took care of him.

We checked him again this morning and he is a little pinker than normal, but he is doing much better. I'm not sure but I think they mixed Desitin with some kind of numbing cream. They apply it really thickly, almost like they are trying to spackle his little butt-crack shut. Still, I don't care how it looks as long as it works.

We have a few tests today, mostly blood tests to check his blood cell counts. We hope his ANC (Absolute Neutrophil Count –

has to do with white blood cells and fighting infections) is fairly high. It can be as high as 1,500 in a perfectly healthy person. The top third (1,000 to 1,500) is great with very little risk of infection. The middle third (500 to 1,000) is OK with some risk, but not too bad. The bottom third (less than 500) is where there is a big threat of infection. If his ANC is less than 500 we have to take some very strong precautions to keep David healthy, and it is unlikely he would be allowed to return to daycare.

We don't know what to expect with this test. There is a medication we'll probably take just before we leave that is supposed to give the ANC a boost, but I don't know how much of a boost is going to be needed.

As we are coming to the end of our stay here at SLCH, I have to take a few moments to say "Thanks" to the wonderful nurses, technicians, doctors and other staff members that we've worked with. I cannot think of a single example of someone being less than professional and kind. There are several examples, however, of people going beyond what I would have expected. Jodi, the nurse/angel on the eighth floor, comes to mind immediately, but there are dozens of people we've worked with that deserve thanks.

Our experience here started with the guy who checked us in. I think his name was Anthony, but it could have been Andrew or Andre. He could have been a cold professional, but instead he took a little time to talk to us and reassure us that we'd made the right choice in coming here. As the first person we met at SLCH he put a good face on the hospital.

At every step of the way people were there to answer questions patiently, to reassure us that things were going to be okay and, perhaps most importantly, to let us know that the swirling emotions we have felt were perfectly normal.

This is an amazing place and these people helped make a dark time in our lives a lot brighter.

Jan. 21, 2008, 11:03 a.m.

We got the blood work back and David's ANC is almost normal. His counts are not that of the average person walking around on the street but they are better than most chemo patients. What a relief!

We are in the process of getting things wrapped up and we'll be leaving the hospital soon. Of course, we'll be back here within a few weeks for the next batch of chemo, but for now we are really happy to head home. Sleeping in our own beds, cooking our own meals (yeah, I'm weird like that), using a remote control for the television set, sitting in chairs that are familiar and comfortable, seeing people we care about even when visiting hours are over. All of these little treats will be ours again soon.

Jan. 21, 2008, 9:04 p.m.

We made it home this afternoon. We were thrilled when we walked in the back door and found that our friends had visited and left us a surprise. Not only did they stock our refrigerator with groceries, but they left us a cake, balloons and a video camera. It was amazing and more than we could have ever asked for.

David is pleased to be home. He grinned from ear-to-ear as we walked around the house and he saw familiar sights. He even giggled a little when he heard our dog, Murray, barking from downstairs.

It's good to be home. We've still got a long road ahead of us but, with the support we've received, we know we can make it. Twice today I've been reminded about the story of David vs. Goliath. Our David is our hero and you can bet your butt that this particular Goliath is goin' down!

The Middle

Jan. 25, 2008 7:17 a.m.

We are taking David in for his next round of chemo treatments today. Luckily, the treatment is here in Champaign so we won't have a long drive ahead of us. We feel so lucky that this doctor is here in town. It is our understanding that he worked very closely with St. Louis Children's Hospital in the past. Our doctors there highly recommend him so we're sure we'll be in good hands. In fact, some of the parents on the oncology floor at SLCH said they live around Champaign and many of them had good things to say about him.

David's been in good spirits since he's been home. Rachel and I have even started getting the hang of giving him his medication through his chest tube. It was creepy at first, and it is still a little nerve-wracking, but it gets easier every day.

Jan. 28, 2008 7:41 p.m.

Today was a tough day for David. He's been very sick to his stomach all day and has had trouble keeping anything down. Also, his throat is getting more and more raw. The doctors at SLCH want us to bring him back to the hospital Tuesday so they can give him some kind of treatment for his throat. I hope it works. The poor little guy just sounds horrible when he cries, only a little more than a squeak.

Still, he seems to be in a relatively good mood. As I'm writing this, he is sitting up, smiling and having fun playing with some of his toys. He just finished a strenuous game of peek-a-boo with a lamp. I'm not sure who won. Yes, I said he played with a lamp. He's a sweet kid but a bit of an odd kid. I guess he takes after his old man after all.

We expect good things tomorrow but we are planning for an overnight stay just in case. We continue to receive tons of support. People overwhelm us with their generosity and their kindness. The smiles, the prayers, and the positive energy coming our way sustain us as we work through David's crisis. We couldn't do it alone. God bless you.

Jan. 30, 2008, 8:08 a.m.

We made a trip to St. Louis Children's Hospital yesterday only to find that David's throat wasn't really a problem anymore. He sounded a lot better, but we wanted to be sure things were okay. It's a good thing we went because we learned that his ANC is about 200, really low, and that he'd have to stay home from daycare until it rises.

We're expecting things to be okay within a few days when David is tested again. We'll learn then if his medication is doing enough to build his ANC

My sister came to St. Louis the other night. She is being tested today to see if she is a good candidate as a liver donor. We are hoping for good news.

Jan. 31, 2008, 3:32 p.m.

I learned an important lesson today. Fat guys shouldn't get too exuberant when they do a happy-dance. It hurts! I think I may have actually pulled a muscle on my shoulder/chest – and it wasn't that good of a dance.

We got some great news recently. David was tested this morning and his ANC rocketed back up to the very healthy range. We had been worried about him and had been keeping him home from daycare because the risk of infection was too high – even with the super-clean environment Dena keeps. We will be able to take him back now. I guess the Neupagen really works.

The other bit of good news is that my sister passed the first rounds of tests to be a living liver donor. She still has another round of fairly invasive tests coming soon, but we're pleased that she made it through this round. She keeps on saying that she isn't doing anything special and that anybody would do the same thing. I don't care what she says. I believe she is being heroic, and I am proud to know her.

Feb. 5, 2008, 11:50 a.m.

We're back in St. Louis today for some relatively routine kidney tests to see how David's kidneys are handling the chemotherapy. I doubt there will be any problems.

We might be staying for a few days for the next round of chemo. I made sub plans and we packed for five days here. However there is a possibility that we could be going home this afternoon. One of the doctors said it is possible that they can arrange for us to take this treatment in Champaign. That would be nice. Instead of four or five full days off for both of us, we can alternate half days off between the two of us.

David has been the same happy, healthy baby that he always is lately. This last round of vincristine chemo he had didn't hurt his throat as much as the first round did. He's a little raspy but nothing compared to how it was two weeks ago.

Feb. 6, 2008, 9:57 a.m.

The tests seemed to go OK for David yesterday. We won't get the results back for a while but he didn't have much trouble with them. I'm glad he has the chest tube. It makes it so easy to administer drugs and to take blood. He had nine blood draws. I can't imagine how hard that would have been if the nurses had to take blood the traditional way each time. They tried to get an IV-type tube in his arm once for the tests but he has little veins (like his Mom) and he screamed so much (like his Dad) that they eventually gave up and used the chest tube.

We did get some good news. This latest round of chemotherapy will be done in Champaign instead of St. Louis. Rachel is spending most of today scheduling that. There was some question as to if our insurance would cover chemo here. I guess it's OK because both hospitals confirmed that we're good-to-go.

We'll be heading back to St. Louis again in about two weeks for one last round of tests before David can be considered officially on the transplant waiting list. I think we'll be getting our pagers.

When the pager goes off it means *they've found a liver* and we have about four hours to get to St. Louis for the surgery.

My sister (the hero) is still undergoing her tests and she still wants to be the donor but the doctors say they'll take whichever liver is best for David at the time.

I learned recently that the PTA at my school is hosting a benefit for us at a roller-skating facility (I promise to fall down several times) and my students organized a Walk-A-Thon benefit for David during school. I know I say if fairly often, but I am continually humbled by the generosity and the positive attitudes people have shown us.

Feb. 10, 2008, 10:15 a.m.

We are back into the hospital (in Champaign) for chemotherapy and an IV fluid drip. We hope the chemo rash isn't as bad this time but, if it is, we have a supply of Butt Paste on hand that we can use immediately to reduce the effects.

We don't expect any problems or complications. The worst thing we expect to happen is that Rachel will be bored during the day.

My heroic sister is already in St. Louis tonight. She is going to continue testing Monday morning to see if she is eligible to be a living liver donor for David. We're keeping our fingers crossed and praying for her.

David had a blood transfusion yesterday because his hemoglobin levels dipped a bit low. On a scale of 1-10 anything lower than an 8 usually will earn David a transfusion. He had a 7.6 yesterday. It was low enough that doctors had to take steps, but not low enough that we had to freak out. Ever since he received the transfusion he's been a wild child. He is waving his arms, screeching, laughing, and generally having way more energy than a (supposedly) sick child should have. I love it.

David is starting to cut his first tooth (for real this time – I think). This one will be a bottom tooth. He has been extra slobbery lately, and we can feel the rough edge of the tooth just under the surface of his gums.

We had some people over to see David the other night. One of our guests was a baby boy only a few months older than David. He was saying, "Da-da-da-da" while they were sitting together. The very next day David started to say it. I have my fingers crossed that David's first word will be "Dad." How cool would that be?!?

Sorry Rachel, the "da" sound is a bit easier to make than the "ma" sound.

Finally, David seems to have learned a new trick. He seems to be giving kisses - on purpose. Sure, they are big, nasty, slobber-filled monsters that make us need to wash our faces, but we love every one of them.

Feb. 13, 2008, 2:12 p.m.

David is doing well with this latest batch of chemotherapy. He had a bit of a rough go with the first day or so of it because he was very sick to his stomach. Last night, however, went well and he only woke up once for a short time.

Rachel has been a real trooper during this time. She's been staying in the hospital with David. She said the nursing staff at our local hospital has been great, similar to those at SLCH which is very high praise.

I've been stuck at home in bed because I've been sick. It's a good thing that I'm sick now instead of in a week. At least David isn't home to catch anything. I'm already on the mend and I hope I'll be able to see my son soon.

The Champaign *News-Gazette* came out to the school Tuesday to interview people about the student council Walk-A-Thon and the PTA benefit. A photographer is going to the hospital today. I guess the story should be out within a few days.

Feb. 14, 2008, 9:09 p.m.

We had both good news and bad news today.

The good news is that David is going to get to come home a bit early. The doctors here in Champaign said he is doing so well on this newest round of chemo that they are going to bump up the schedule a bit. Hoo-rah!

The bad news was a bit of a shock today. We learned that my sister has been eliminated as a potential liver donor. She has said that she felt certain she'd be the one to save David. She said she'd figured out what her purpose in life was, so now she's heartbroken by this news. While we are disappointed with this news we are in no way disappointed with her. Her willingness to make a sacrifice for David is not lessened because she was unable to do so. We know that she would have done anything within her power to be the donor (just as so many other people would have done), but it wasn't in the cards. We love her, respect her, and I am damn proud to be her brother. She sets the definition for heroic and for Christian in my book. God bless her.

We'll be heading back to St. Louis Children's Hospital in a few days for additional tests. While we are there we will talk with the transplant team to find out what our next step should be. I imagine that they are going to go back to the list of potential donors that called in last month to find the next best candidate. In the meantime we will probably get the emergency pagers so they can let us know if a suitable cadaver donor shows up.

Feb. 15, 2008, 7:22 p.m.

DAVID IS HOME!

Can ya tell that I'm a bit excited?!? David made it home early today. and it was such a great feeling to know I was going to get to see him, hold him, and play with him all evening. How cool is it to hear a baby laugh? Yeah, I know I kinda sound like a pansy right about now, but I couldn't get enough of that laugh of his tonight. I don't think I put him down for more than five minutes every hour he was awake (that could be why it is only about 7:30 p.m. and he's already been asleep for about 20 minutes. I wore him out).

David wasn't supposed to come home before about 9 p.m. tomorrow, but the doctors said he was doing so well on his latest round of chemotherapy that they were able to speed things up and release him early.

Rachel is taking a well-deserved night off with some friends tonight. They are eating Italian food, having a glass of wine, and letting Rachel enjoy the fact that she's not sleeping on a hospital couch/bench tonight. Rachel has been a trooper this whole week. It hasn't been easy being the only parent staying with David 24/7 in the hospital. I've been sick and I wasn't allowed in without a mask, and only then for short periods of time.

Feb. 18, 2008, 12:30 p.m.

We made it to St. Louis with plenty of time to spare today. I guess it wasn't quite necessary to give myself almost five hours travel time for a three hour trip. In my defense I was a bit worried about weather.

We're scheduled to meet with doctors for tests in a few minutes and then we meet with the transplant team after that. We don't expect to be at SLCH too long today and we are fully expecting to be home tonight. We packed an overnight bag just in case, but we don't expect to have to use it.

I've had a lot of time lately to think about the Walk-A-Thon that the school held a few days ago to raise money for us. Everyone I spoke with that day had nothing but positive, uplifting things to say. Some offered prayers, others offered a few kind words, and a valuable few offered jokes I can use here at the hospital, but everyone had something to say that helped us.

Perhaps the best thing that happened to me that day was seeing the looks on the faces of my students. I could tell that they all understood what they were doing and why they were doing it. Sure, they were having fun talking with friends and enjoying themselves, but they didn't seem to forget the real reason for their actions. I had a few opportunities to talk to some of these students one-on-one. Their support and the things they had to say meant a lot to me.

These were not the comments of students kissing up to a teacher or just saying something they thought I wanted to hear. These were students who cared deeply about us. They were proud that they were able to do something to help. I always say that I am proud of my students, but I am extra proud as I think of their selflessness in recent weeks. Whether it is raising money through the Walk-A-Thon or simply being there with a kind word and a smile when I needed it my kids haven't let me down. If only I could get them to do their reading homework I'd be all set.

Feb. 18, 2008, 6:47 p.m.

Wow, time really flies when you're having ... well, whatever it is that we're having today.

Actually, we had a good trip to St. Louis. We're home now and we had some good news while we were there.

David's doctor poked and prodded on him a bit and pronounced that the chemotherapy is doing everything they had hoped it would do. The tumor has shrunk and David's liver has hardened somewhat – both of which are good things apparently. I would have thought a harder liver was a bad thing but I would have been wrong (first time for everything).

We're still waiting for the results of David's blood test. They'll have that for us in the morning so he'll be at daycare for a while. If the numbers come back low, Rachel will pick him up and spend the day with him at home.

We learned that the tumor is almost certainly the kind we had hoped it would be and that, genetically speaking, things aren't going to get worse. We are going ahead with the liver transplant procedures.

The doctors said we are officially on the liver waiting list and we could hear something as early as this week. Most likely, however, it will probably be a few weeks. If we are on the waiting list longer than a month, the doctors will put David on Status One, which means they open up the donor search full-blast and nationwide. When this happens we could get a liver within hours. The doctors said the longest they've had someone wait once they reach Status One is a week.

We got to stop by on the ninth floor after talking to the doctors so we could visit with Taylor. She's a girl that was in the room next to ours during our last long stay in SLCH. She's a sweet kid (reminds me a lot of some of my students) who is in fifth grade and really misses being in school. We spent a little time talking to her and her mother, checking in with them. She tends to have a lot of longer hospital stays so they appreciate having a visitor who isn't wearing a lab coat.

Hopefully things go well with her this visit and her numbers stay high.

Feb. 25, 2008 5:04 p.m.

Today has been something of a dark day for us. Not horrible, but kinda dark. We learned that our next chance at a living donor, David's godfather, has been rejected. I've said this before about my sister when she tried to be a donor, and I'll definitely say it about David's godfather – his efforts were heroic. His willingness to put himself on the line and potentially risk his life to save my son is a heroic thing. He is a credit to his family and we are proud to know him and to call him part of our family.

I know he is disappointed. We are disappointed too, but not in him.

The day was doubly dark because we learned that David still isn't officially on the donor waiting list even though we thought he'd be on the list a week ago. There is still another test the doctors need to run before things can be made official. This means the potential waiting time is still five weeks or more. Yeah, it's only one extra week and who knows when the right liver would have come in. Still, it's a bit of a let down.

Because of the timing of things it is becoming increasingly difficult to find a living donor. There were plenty of people who were willing to step up to do anything they could for David. Their efforts are still appreciated and it is still possible that one of them will be the right person. However, because the testing process takes so long it is looking more likely that we'll need to rely on a cadaver donor.

Intellectually, I know that giving a donation and saving David's life might be just the thing a grieving family needs to give their tragedy meaning. Maybe it will help them make sense of their situation and bring them some measure of peace. Still, emotionally I have some problems with it. I keep going back to the fact that someone else has to go through the unthinkable so that my family can avoid a similar fate. That's just something I'll have to get over. This kind of negative thinking doesn't help anything, but that's where I am right now. I'll be fine once I get my head on straight and can get a little distance from today's news. It's just a little too fresh for me at this point.

I hope I'm not depressing anyone. That really isn't my intention. I've told myself throughout this experience that I wanted to write as truthfully as I could about both the good and the bad. Ultimately I'm sure that things will be OK for David. I'm just thinking today about that other family. I don't know who they are going to be, but I hope their gift will help make sense of their tragedy. I'm going to be praying for them.

If you are reading this, please take out your driver's license, sign the back and talk to your family about your decision. Who knows who you might be saving.

Feb. 28, 2008, 1:46 p.m.

We're back at SLCH today for a CT scan. This is (hopefully)

the last step before we can be put on the transplant waiting list. We've heard that before, but we feel pretty good about it this time.

David just left with the doctors to perform the scan. He's in a good mood, a little hungry and sleepy, but still in a good mood. He might have a sore throat after the procedure because of the breathing tube that they may have to put in, but he should be fine. This isn't an invasive procedure.

We didn't expect to have to be here today. I honestly believe someone made a bit of a mistake with our schedule and forgot to plan for this scan. Then, because they have to have the scan before the next chemo treatment, we had to make quick plans to come down to St. Louis. It wouldn't have been a big deal at all except for the fact that we have the Kenwood [Elementary School] PTA benefit at the roller-rink tonight.

We should still be able to make the benefit, but we might be a bit late. At least one of us (probably David, but maybe Daddy) will be a little cranky. "Lucky Mommy," says Rachel dryly from beside me as I type this.

I'm going to drop off letters my students have written to Taylor today. I hope the letters can cheer her up. She seems like such a sweet kid and, because she's about the same age as my students, they have taken up her cause and they want to make her stay here as happy as possible. Maybe she'll even want to be pen-pals with some of the kids. We'll see.

I'm in a much better place today and I'm back to being my old self. I'm looking at things from a better perspective and that helps.

I'm not going to say that the idea of a cadaver donor is really appealing to me, but I'm much more accepting of the idea now.

We're moving forward and staying positive. I'm looking forward to Skateland tonight. I'll probably fall at least once (dramatically), and I'll be a terror in the laser tag area.

Feb. 28, 2008, 10:03 p.m.

We are back from the hospital and the fund raiser. It's been a long but good day and both stops today, while very different, were just what we needed.

The hospital provided some welcome good news. The CT scan showed that David's tumor was shrinking, and he is responding well to the chemotherapy. We figured this already based on what one of the doctors said after David's last examination, but it's nice to have photographic confirmation. This means that David is officially on the transplant waiting list (we have already received our confirmation phone call). We originally thought the transplant could be within five weeks, and it still could be, but we (Rachel and I, not the doctors) failed to take into account how David will be temporarily off the list while he is getting chemo. This could add some time to the wait, but not much. We could have a new liver very soon.

The unexpected good news at the hospital was that one area of the tumor that had particularly troubled the doctors has disappeared entirely. There was a lump near David's adrenal gland that was bothersome but the chemo worked so well that it has shrunk completely back into the liver.

While the trip to the hospital was good for David's health, the trip to Skateland Skating Rink was good for our spirits. (Is that as corny to read as it is to type? I don't care, that's how it feels.) The turnout was amazing. There were hundreds of people there to wish us well and to support us in a rough time.

While we are grateful to everyone who attended, called us, wrote us letters, visited our web site, prayed for us and generally gave us good wishes – I found it especially gratifying to see so many former and current students of mine. That was very touching and came at a time when I needed some cheering up.

I always end each school year by reminding my students that, while they may not be in my class anymore, they will always be "Mr. Weber's Kids." Well, my kids (past, present and future) came through for me again tonight. It meant a lot to me that they were there.

Feb. 29, 2008, 6:27 p.m.

I don't have anything earth-shattering to report today, but I have something on the lighter-side of liver transplantation.

We received our pager Thursday and it was my job to call in to SLCH today to schedule a test page to make sure things were working. The battery was good and the volume was high enough. Somehow, the ornery switch was flipped today and I turned into the "Little Boy Who Cried Liver!"

I need to preface this story a bit. I've tried to prepare my students for the possibility that the pager could go off at any time and I'll have to leave quickly. They know how important this is to my family and they have all promised to keep themselves under control if I have to leave suddenly one day. I've got a good bunch of kids this year.

Well, as I was setting up the test page today the woman on the other end of the phone call said she had everything set up and that the pager would go off in about 30-45 seconds. I admit that I was a bit of a jerk here, but I couldn't help myself. When I heard her say I had a few seconds I went out into the hallway where one of my students was waiting for the after-school program to start.

The test page went off, the student looked up at me in surprise, and I scrambled to pull the pager out of my pocket. I checked out the page's screen for a second and then bolted into a dead run down the hall - as if I had just received an emergency page saying that we had a liver. The girl in the hall (a sweet girl who should have known better than to fall for anything I'm doing) obviously thought that this was "The Real Thing."

When I came back around the corner she was just on the edge of a panic – "Was it? Is it? WELL!?!"

I couldn't keep a straight face and she knew immediately that she'd been tricked. To her credit she wasn't too mad.

Oh, I live for those moments.

March 7, 2008, 8:18 a.m.

We had some fairly good news last night that counteracted the bad news we had received yesterday morning. David is going to be able to go to our local hospital today to start his next round of chemo. Originally we had thought that his platelet count was too low - not dangerously low, just too low for chemo - but somewhere, someone had made a mistake and David's numbers were fine. He'll be in in the hospital for the next five days.

If we hadn't had chemo here in Champaign this weekend, we were going to have to go spend almost all of next week getting it in St. Louis. It would have been a nightmare to get things organized at school (the week after mandatory state tests, the week report cards come out, and the last week before a break is not the best time to be gone) but I don't have to worry about that now.

I was so pleased to hear that we could stay up here that I didn't even get angry about the original mistake.

David is doing fine. It's a blessing that he doesn't ever seem to act like a sick kid. He doesn't cry and whine and he is really getting into playing peek-a-boo and being tickled. This would have been so much more difficult if he didn't have this great attitude.

I've always said that David would beat this thing with a smile. It looks like he inherited more than just a wave in his hair from my grandfather. My grandpa, Don, had a great life-affirming attitude. That's why he always was and still is one of my heroes. David seems to have picked up great-grandpa's attitude.

David is still sleeping through the night. We were worried that the first few days he slept all night could have been just because he was so tired from being in the hospital. It could have been a fluke.

Thankfully, he is still sleeping, which means that Rachel and I are sleeping for the first time in almost nine months.

March 9, 2008, 3:28 p.m.

David is on his second day in chemotherapy today. He's doing fairly well and he's only spit up a few times. That means he is either getting more used to the chemo or they have used a slightly different blend that is easier on him. Either way I'm pleased that he seems to be handling things well.

He has stayed in a good mood throughout this visit too. He's a little irritable at times. Maybe he's bored. I know that his parents are bored, so I guess he's probably feeling that way too.

One of our closest friends, David's daycare provider, came out last night to give us a break for dinner. It was great to get away for a little while. We went out to Papa George's and we really liked it. We hadn't been there before but we both like Greek food so it was a little adventure. Our friend said she wants to come back out for a bit tonight too. We'll try to take it easy on her and get back quickly. We don't want to impose too much. I think she misses David. Before cancer she was used to having him with her every day. She is like a member of the family.

March 10, 2008, 10:07 p.m.

David is having an MRI Tuesday morning to make sure the cancer hasn't spread to his brain and I have to admit to having a few dark thoughts tonight. This is one of those rough "What If?"

moments that are so hard throughout this process. Today, however, was a little different than some of my other dark days because I was reminded again today of so many positive things that have come out of this experience - things I should be (and am) thankful for.

I was sitting in the hospital alone with David this evening. Rachel had gone home because she wasn't feeling very well and she needed a break. There was a knock on the door and one of our best friends walked in unexpectedly. She knew that hospital times could be tough, and she wanted to stop by to try to keep my spirits up.

We didn't talk about anything of earth-shattering importance; just some school stuff, some baby stuff, and some family stuff. It was the same kind of chit-chat that was happening in coffee shops all around the country at that exact moment, but that nothing-special-conversation was actually very special because it was just what I needed.

During her visit, we had a phone call and a text message from two other friends who were also checking in to be sure everything was okay. It meant a lot to me to know that these people were there for me at a time that could have been pretty dark. I'm thankful for them and for all of the other wonderful friends and family members who have made gestures (both large and small) at just the right moments throughout this entire process.

Later that night I was walking around the floor of the hospital on some errand and I noticed a young boy, maybe seven or eight years old hanging out in the play room. He was clearly uncomfortable and was obviously going through some problems. I became thankful that, if all goes according to plan, David will likely not remember any of this process. That's a blessing.

As I drove home from the hospital tonight I reflected on how there seemed to be no end to the people who have stepped up to volunteer as living liver donors. The latest is the Kenwood music teacher. I was thankful to have her in my life before David got sick because she's always been a good friend, but thankful doesn't even begin to express how I feel about her and the others who called in to the hotline not knowing if their kindness would put them at risk. I've used the word "heroic" quite a bit, but I have a hard time thinking of any other word to describe these people.

Most of all I realized last night how thankful I am to have had David in my life at all. As I hugged him goodbye and kissed him on his head (the way I always do at night before he goes to bed) I was stuck by how proud I am of him and how he's holding up. He is living his life without fear. I don't know if I would have the strength he's showing if our positions were reversed, and that's one of the myriad of reasons I am thankful for him.

Clearly I hope and pray for the best outcome but, if the unthinkable should happen, I'll still be thankful for the time I've had with him. As utterly devastated as I'd be and as hard as this is to think about right now, I know that at least part of me will understand that I'm a better person because of him. Regardless of the results of this test or any future tests or surgeries I know that I've had a touch of perfection in my life because of that boy. I see that perfection every time he smiles and I hear it every time he laughs. If there is a

Heaven it is filled with those two things.

March 15, 2008, 9:05 p.m.

This isn't going to be a usual entry. I wish I had some kind of update to provide but I don't. We had the MRI Tuesday morning to see if the cancer had spread to David's brain. So far we haven't heard any word from the doctors one way or the other. I have to assume that things are fine. No news is good news, right?

My instincts (from all of my many long years of fatherhood, haha) tell me that, if something was wrong, the doctors would have called us right away. That they haven't called has to be a good thing. At least I hope that it is.

One cool thing that happened during that hospital trip is that we got to see the teeth that David is developing. One of the nurses showed us the MRI pictures on her computer (another reason I think things are fine – they had the pictures that morning and have had all this time to look at them). She quickly flipped through the pictures of brain images that I wouldn't understand and found the pictures of David's face. We could clearly see where several teeth are forming just below the gum line. It was really cool! My son was smiling at me with teeth that haven't even come out yet.

March 17, 2008, 5:18 p.m.

Happy St. Patrick's Day! There's an old Irish blessing I'd like to share with you today. "May the wind at your back not be from the corned beef and cabbage you had on St. Patrick's Day." I love that joke.

Well, back to reality. We are in Carle Hospital today for a (hopefully) very brief stay. David's platelet count was low again after today's blood test. We're in for the afternoon and early evening for a transfusion. We should be home by mid-evening at the latest. Today's procedure is nothing dangerous. It just means we have a boring afternoon watching hospital TV.

Why can't the hospital afford good TV stations? Don't we pay thousands of dollars per day to rent these rooms? I wouldn't pay that much for a hotel that didn't have HBO.

David's ANC (the important blood count we usually talk about) was also very low -- around 200. Babies are considered normal if they have 1,500 or more. When David had his test done on Thursday his ANC was through the roof, and now it is around 200. Wow, that's a huge drop in such a short period of time.

The ANC dropping is something a little more serious than the platelet count, but only slightly. All the low ANC means at this point is that we have to be extra careful to keep David germ free. This should be relatively easy because he is staying home with me this week. As long as we keep him away from sick people (I don't count - I'm only sick in the head and that isn't contagious) and are extra careful to wash our hands with the sanitizing lotion we should be fine.

The low ANC is a bit of a bummer because it means that we have to stay inactive on the transplant list a few days longer than we had hoped. Rachel and I both had the feeling that we'd be getting a call from St. Louis Children's Hospital about midweek telling us that they found us a liver. Oh well, we will get one eventually. I'm not worried about that, but it would have been a cool story to tell later on ..." Well son, your mother and I both had a feeling that good things would happen that week ..." and everybody knows how much I love a good story.

No biggie. We'll be on the active list again very soon. Who knows? Perhaps, after the next blood test, we can still get the call before the end of the week and our predictions will still come true.

If not, we can always claim that Leap Day threw us off a bit and that we really meant that the call would come next week ... yeah, that's the ticket! (I'm sitting here at the computer doing a lame Jon Lovitz impression based on his SNL character The Pathological Liar. I'm such a goof.) And our nurse will look just like Morgan Fairchild!

March 19, 2008, 10:35 p.m.

I've just started reading a new book by a cancer survivor. It's a realistic look at cancer through the eyes of someone who's been there. The author talks about the "wow" moments of cancer: the moments that are scary, the moments that are funny, and the moments that are just odd.

The first few chapters are, duh, about how he found out that he had cancer. He said his diagnosis was not just unlikely, it was miraculous because he hadn't been to a doctor in years. He had noticed a small lump on his arm, about the size of a bug bite or a really big pimple but beneath the skin. He instinctively knew something was wrong and went to see his doctor.

That story got me thinking that I hadn't ever really discussed here how we found out about David's cancer. I would have to call it miraculous too.

Rachel and I had both been ill with a mild virus. It was the usual stuff that I don't need to go into here. Suffice to say I was pin wheeling at one point (if you don't know what that means, you are probably better off). A few days after we got over being sick, David started showing some similar symptoms. He was vomiting a lot, loose poop, cranky. All the usual stuff. But his symptoms seemed to last a little longer than ours did.

At one point Rachel (God bless motherly instinct) said, "If he vomits one more time, I'm going to call the doctor for an appointment."

Well, he did vomit one more time. Exactly one more time. After that one time he didn't show a single sign of being sick. Still, Rachel made the appointment and made sure that we kept it even though David didn't show any more symptoms of the flu.

While we were there, thinking all along that we were wasting our time, our pediatrician was feeling David's stomach the way they always do when a baby has been vomiting. He noticed a hard ridge just below the ribcage on David's right side that shouldn't be there. This ridge bothered him enough that he said he thought we should have it checked out, "Just in case."

In the past I thought that the phrase "just in case" from a doctor usually meant that the doctor had a payment on his new boat he needed to make and I would be handling that bill. Well, I can't say that I won't think that kind of thought again but I'll darn sure follow through with the doctor's request.

We scheduled the tests and found out that David had worse problems than just the flu. You know most of the rest of the story.

One thing you don't know is that, on the day our doctor suggested the test, he also told us that he was planning to retire at the end of that month. Can you believe that I was actually a little ticked at the guy when he gave us that bit of news? How dare he take us on as clients/patients only a few months ago when he knew he was going to retire soon?!? What an inconvenience this was going to be. Now we'll have to find a doctor all over again after searching for quite a while to find him. Why would he do this to us?!?

DERP! God help me, sometimes I'm just not that bright.

If this man hadn't taken us on as clients/patients I don't know what would have happened. Would some other doctor have noticed the hard ridge? Would anybody else have taken the risk of annoying/scaring new parents by making them go through the, possibly, unnecessary tests and run the risk of losing these clients/patients? What if this new doctor didn't like boats and didn't need to make a payment? (Okay, that last one was a joke but you can see where I'm going with this, right?)

Who's to say that things would have worked out this way if we had been with anyone other than him? I hope he knows what he did for us. I hope he knows that every laugh, cry, burp or sigh from

David is a "thank you" for paying attention to your job when someone else might have checked out.

Regardless of how David's cancer ultimately turns out, I have to say that I think this doctor went out on a win. He gave David a fighting chance against cancer and for that I am forever in his debt. Maybe I'll be able to pay him back someday. I know. I'll buy the beer when he takes me out on his boat.

March 21, 2008, 3:36 p.m.

We got the MRI results back Thursday and everything is fine. It's a strange feeling getting this kind of news. I never really thought that the cancer had spread but, when I heard the doctor actually say the words, I let go of a breath that I hadn't even realized I'd been holding. A wave of tension that I hadn't known I'd been storing up suddenly released and the world was somehow a better place.

Yeah, I know that sounds corny but I'm like that sometimes. Deal with it.

The other news that day was only so-so, but not a big deal. David's blood counts were still really low. His ANC had actually fallen even farther than before. It was down to 104. His hemoglobin count was also fairly low. There isn't any danger as long as we keep a close eye on David and make sure he doesn't come in contact with any sick people. He basically doesn't have an immune system right now so even mild colds could be very dangerous.

The doctor said David's monocytes (I hope I'm using the right word - it was medical talk and I was REALLY tired that day from being Mr. Mom all week) were very high. The monocytes spike just before the other blood cells begin rapid development so we expect his ANC and his hemoglobin counts to be very good by the weekend.

We'll get another blood test on Monday but things should be fine well before then.

Hopefully, Monday's test will be good enough that we can stop giving David some of his medications. He has to be off the medication for a few days before we can be on the active waiting list for the transplant. If all goes well we should be on the active list by mid-to-late next week.

Almost The End

Author's Note:

I want to warn parents about this next part. Up until now my journey has been similar to what many of you have had. We've probably shared many of the same feelings, the same hopes and fears. While every cancer is different, just like every child is different, there are many things we've had in common.

After this point, we will, hopefully, have different stories. You should tighten up your emotional armor as you continue reading. We love and respect the doctors, nurses, and other healthcare professionals with whom we worked. Despite their best efforts our outcome wasn't good.

I'm not saying that you should avoid reading this next part, but I'll understand if you want to skip it for a while.

March 28, 2008, 6:08 p.m.

I didn't want to have to write this. We got the results of the CT scan today. It was "inconclusive." That's medical jargon for "we don't really know what's up."

The good news was that the chemotherapy seems to be working. The tumor on David's liver has shrunk again. This is great. It means we haven't been in the hospital and going through all of this for nothing.

The odd news, however, is that the CT shows some unusual

spots on David's lung and on his adrenal gland. The doctors aren't sure what this means. It could be nothing. It could be that he has some slightly enlarged blood vessels or some other minor thing that doesn't mean anything. With my luck it could be a thumbprint on the lenses of the CT camera. (Yeah, I know it isn't really a camera but work with me, people. I'm grasping at straws here.)

The other alternative is that the cancer has spread beyond his liver. Ultimately, this means that David's prognosis isn't very good and that we could lose our son.

Wow, that was hard to write.

I don't think that's what's going to happen, and the doctors don't think that is what's going to happen. The doctors said they think it is strange that the tumor on/in David's liver is shrinking and yet two other spots, both of which are being hit by the same chemotherapy that is working on the liver, could be growing?!? It doesn't make sense.

Still, we are checking it out just in case because the slim possibility exists that this could be really bad. I guess that is eating me up inside. When I got the news today, I was on my way to the mall. I was going to get something to eat at the food court (love that double-meat chicken from the Japanese place). I sat down at a table with my lunch and, because the newspaper rack was sold out, I spent a little time people watching.

It started off okay. I saw packs of teenage girls running back and forth with whatever the hot new gossip was and there were plenty of *Cops*-worthy arguments going on around me. Still, in retrospect, I probably shouldn't have gone people watching so soon after getting the news. I spent most of the time seeing fathers and sons enjoying themselves at the mall.

First there was the dad who was holding a three-year-old boy on the merry-go-round. Clearly, this was one of the first rides, if not THE first ride that this kid had ever taken. He was enthralled. There were big grins on both of their faces. Next, I saw the guy carrying a four- or five-year old on his shoulders. The boy was enjoying his special time with dad. He loved hanging out at the mall while his dad was trying not to get kicked in the face whenever his son got too excited.

There was a guy in his mid-fifties who was taking his college-aged son out to buy something that the kid probably needed before heading back to school. I saw a man making fun of his teenage boy about girls, the young man obviously mortified to have to have this conversation with his oh-so-uncool father, especially in public.

I sat there for more than an hour, just watching guys and their sons. All of these men were just spending the day doing what fathers all over the world were doing. I just sat there feeling more and more maudlin and wondering if I was ever going to get to do those things.

I know, it's kind of lame for me to be thinking about myself and my own issues at this time, but that's what I was doing and I won't apologize for it.

Did those men realize what they had going for them? Did they appreciate watching their boys at those exact moments in their lives? Were they remembering what things were like when their sons were younger or were they wrapped up in what was going on at that exact moment? Did those dads ever think about how things could be different and that they might not be so lucky?

I know. I was probably only seeing the things that I was looking for. There were probably plenty of other guys there who were not having those "postcard moments" with their kids. They weren't taking time to appreciate their sons. They weren't talking. They weren't playing and they weren't riding the carousel. And, yes, I appreciate the irony that as I was thinking those thoughts, my own son was in daycare because I had a bunch of stuff to do and it was easier to get things done without carrying around a baby.

I don't know what's going to happen in the next few weeks or months. I know that we're off of the active transplant list and that we probably won't have any test results for well more than a week. We're going to be back in for about a week's worth of chemotherapy in a few days. The doctors want to take another CT scan and possibly an MRI so they can get a better idea of what's going on.

To me, that means I've got at least ten days, probably more than two weeks, of wondering, "What if?" and hoping that, in a few years, some other dad will get to see me enjoying a day with my son at the mall.

March 31, 2008 10:41 a.m.

I'm not where I thought I'd be today. We had to delay chemotherapy a little while so the latest blood tests could be read. At worst, this puts us off the active-status transplant list for an extra day and, at this point, we're pretty used to that.

With our earlier predictions (mine and Rachel's, not anyone with any real medical training) we thought the transplant would probably happen sometime near the end of March and certainly by the middle of April. Oops! I guess we undershot that mark by a bit. Oh well. It will happen sooner or later and, as long as David is healthy and happy while we wait, we aren't going to be too concerned about when things will finally happen.

Despite the strangeness of the CT scan from last week, we were determined to have a good weekend and David was more than willing to play along. At this point worrying doesn't do any good and it could, in fact, cause some damage. Worrying would only take away from the possible good times that we could be having, so we all do our best to avoid stressing out.

For example, let me give a quick rundown of how yesterday went for David: Wake up. Diaper change. Get dressed. Laugh. Laugh. Jump in the bouncer. Laugh. Whine. EAT! Laugh. Laugh. Nap (too short). Diaper change. Laugh. Tickle fight with Dad. Laugh. Laugh. Eat. Snuggle with Mom. Laugh … well, you get the picture.

Overall, it was a fantastic weekend. David was in a phenomenal mood that was completely infectious. This is just about the only time the word "infectious" is considered a good thing at our house lately. We're hoping this mood lasts through the coming week when we're in the hospital. It makes that time away from home go a lot easier when he's feeling happy.

April 2, 2008, 1:32 p.m.

We talked to our local doctor yesterday, and he said he
believes the odd spots on the CT scan are probably vascular and
have nothing to do with cancer. He wasn't 100 percent certain, but he
is fairly confident that further tests will prove that the spots are
nothing to worry about.

Whew!

We are still in Carle hospital getting more chemotherapy
("We?" I think David might argue this point. "We" aren't getting
chemo. HE is. That kid will argue over the smallest semantic detail).
We, and this time I mean "we," will get out earlier than originally
thought. Possibly as soon as tonight. It would be nice to be home
tonight because Rachel is exhausted. David doesn't want to be held
by anyone other than Mommy, so she's been doing most of the work.

I think this is the same type of chemo that David had the first
time, down in St. Louis. I hope it isn't the one that made his hair fall
out. It's just starting to come back in. I do know that one of the drugs
he got last night was the nasty one nicknamed "Red Devil" because
of the red pee. I'm so glad they warned me about that one. I would
have freaked out if I'd have pulled open a diaper and found that it
was soaked with red. The drug looks kind of like ruby red grapefruit
juice as it is going in. Come to think of it, the drug looks kind of like
ruby red grapefruit juice as it's coming out too.

I'm at home right now doing a load of chemo-laundry after an
unfortunate breakfast incident. Let's just say that I was really glad

that David only wanted Mommy to hold him. Otherwise, it would have been my clothes in the washer right now. Ick.

On the way home I came to a realization (it's funny how so many of those happen in my truck on the way back from a hospital visit). I should never listen to country music after a chemo session. I'm usually pretty keyed up emotionally during these times and I fall for every cheap, manipulative song writing technique that they can come up with. I end up trying not to look like a complete wuss, blinking back tears and swallowing that lump in my throat at stoplights.

Sure, I know what they're doing and the tricks the songwriters are using, but I buy into it every single time. "Don't Blink," "Live Like You Were Dying," and "Earl's Gotta Die" (Okay, not that last one.) Man, I hate those guys right about now.

April 12, 2008, 8:29 p.m.

I had an odd experience the other day. Not bad, just odd enough to make me think about it over and over for the past few days.

I was bringing in a load of groceries and I saw a woman walking across the street. She seemed to notice me, doing a kind of double take before walking slowly across the street. I wasn't certain she was coming my way until she reached my side of the road.

She walked about halfway up the driveway and said, "Do you have a son? A baby boy named David?" It was my turn to do a double take because I was sure I'd never met the woman before, at least not recently enough that she could have met David and I at the same time.

I told her yes and she walked a bit closer so we could have a conversation without having to yell from one end of the driveway to the other. She told me her name and how she knew about our situation and that all of the people at her church were praying for David every day.

I'm ashamed that I cannot remember her name or that of her church, but in my defense I was taken off guard. She asked how David was doing and how we were all holding up. I told her that everyone was doing as well as we could possibly expect under the circumstances.

We talked a little bit more and, before too long, it was obvious that the woman had said everything she wanted to say, but there was a hesitancy before she left. She had wanted to offer some words of encouragement and comfort and, after doing that, it seemed almost as if she wanted to say something else or maybe even give me a hug, but thought it would be weird because we were strangers (it probably would have been weird, come to think of it). Still, our conversation had an unfinished feel to it.

I guess the closest comparison I can offer is meeting up with an old girlfriend unexpectedly on the street. You exchange a few pleasantries and catch each other up on what you've been doing and where mutual friends are.

When the conversation ends it feels strange that you both walked away without the kiss or hug that marked the ending of almost all of your conversations while you were dating. There is a palpable something missing from what you used to have and you are not sure what you should do or say to fill that gap so you just nod.

I've had a few days to think about this, and I imagine the unfinished feeling was pretty accurate. I've had a lot of conversations like that one in the past few months. People seem to want to say "the right thing" and often can't think of what that might be so they let the silence hang on just a touch too long – a pregnant pause before they formally end things and walk on. They usually look me almost in the eyes, make a slightly sad face, nod and then turn away.

I guess I just wanted to say that I understand there are things that are hard to say, things people can't always say, things that almost got said during the pauses. I've felt that way too. Maybe the important thing is that you tried to say something. You tried to help in a situation where there really isn't anything you can do other than offer support.

To all of those people: thanks for the things that you've said and the things that you've almost said during those pauses.

We'll be heading back to St. Louis in a few days. Doctors there want to take another CT scan and an MRI. Hopefully, this will help them get to the bottom of whatever those previous spots were. I'm betting (and so are most of our doctors) that the spots are simply blood vessels that were irritated and enlarged by the recent chemotherapy. Unfortunately there is a small chance that the cancer could have spread. We're trying to rule that out.

The tests should let us know if we have to continue with the chemo. They should also let us know when we can go back to active status on the transplant waiting list.

I know that we have to be patient and that we want everything to be completely right for David. We certainly don't want to rush anything with this transplant and take the chance of making a mistake. Still, this waiting is starting to wear on everybody involved. Don't get me wrong, we're still trying to be very positive and upbeat but it takes a little more effort today than it did two months ago.

It's probably our own fault. We heard the doctors say that it would be about a month and we got our hopes up. I guess we weren't paying close attention to the fact that what the doctors were really saying was that it would be about a month of active status. We go to inactive status whenever David gets chemotherapy and for about a week or more after the chemo. We also go inactive whenever David's blood counts get too low or whenever the doctors have any kind of question as to what certain test results mean.

Ultimately, we've spent more time inactive lately than we have active. It's hard not to be anxious knowing what's at stake. Nerves get frayed and tempers flare more often than they used to (I have to admit that the temper problem is usually mine). We'll get through it. What other choice do we have?

David still seems determined to be a regular boy (Pinocchio, anyone?) during this process. Doctors warned us that his development could be delayed a little bit because of all the hospital stays, but he is still on schedule.

David started crawling this week. It's still a bad version of an army low-crawl but he's getting around. He seems so happy when he's on the move. It's like a light switch came on and he suddenly realized that he can go get whatever he wants on his own. It's great for almost everyone in the family to see. I say "almost" because Murray (our old pug dog – yeah, our girl dog has a boy name) is usually what David wants to go after and she's not too pleased about it. She has to keep getting up from her comfortable spot and move to a different part of the room. About ten minutes later (that's how long it takes David to get across the room) she has to get up and move again.

David also seems to be teething again. Rachel thinks a top front tooth is coming in and that David is having a bit of trouble with this one. He's a little more fussy lately and he has had some truly atrocious diapers so I'm betting she's right. We had such an easy time with the first two that we might have fooled ourselves into thinking hing would be easy. WRONG!

April 15, 2008, 8:50 a.m.

We learned last night that David has some kind of growth on his lungs and his adrenal gland. The things we thought were probably enlarged or irritated blood vessels were actually small tumors that have been aggressively growing for the past few weeks.

We're back to SLCH later this week for a biopsy. The doctors will test the tissue to see whether or not the growths are benign or malignant.

If the growths are malignant, it is unlikely that we will be able to arrange a liver transplant. Even if they are benign, there is a possibility that the doctors will rule out a transplant because certain types of benign growths can cause additional problems later on. The doctors want to give the transplants to the patients with the best chances for positive outcomes.

If we do not get the liver transplant it will mean that David will most likely die.

God damn, that was hard to write.

As I'm writing this I'm having a hard time reconciling my two realities.

One reality is that David seems like a perfectly healthy and happy (albeit bald) 10-month-old baby boy. He's right next to me in his bouncer, jumping around, shaking his toys and talking up a storm. He'll pause every now and then to take a break and he'll grin up at me showing off both of his teeth. Most of the time, however, his eyes are glued to the dog and his smiles are all for Murray.

My other reality is that this beautiful, perfect little boy could be taken from me very soon, and there is absolutely nothing I can do about it. I'm completely helpless. I'm wondering if my son will get to have his first birthday.

I guess I've prepared myself for the possibility that the surgery might not be successful. I know that there could be complications from such a major operation. He could develop an infection, or he could face organ rejection issues once the surgery is done. I think I'm ready for that (well, as ready as a parent can be for such things) but I feel blindsided by this latest news. I never thought for a moment that we might not be able to have the surgery and that I'd have to watch as the cancer slowly takes its toll.

In January when we first got the news about David's cancer, I did something that I hadn't done in a long time. I went to the hospital chapel and I prayed. I knelt down and I cried and I said I didn't think I was strong enough to deal with this. The next morning I woke up and, somehow, I knew I would be strong enough to get through at least the next few weeks.

Last night I sat in my truck after making a late-night run to the pharmacy for David's medication. I prayed again, I cried again, and I said that I didn't know if I was strong enough to get through this. This morning I woke up and I still feel like I won't be strong enough to get through it if David is taken from me.

April 17, 2008, 10:52 a.m.

We'll be coming home today and we'll get to sleep in our own beds. That's the good news.

We don't really know anything more today than we knew earlier this week. There is a growth near David's right adrenal gland. The surgeon said he looked at the scans this morning and he didn't know for certain if it was a growth on the gland or if it was something extending off of the tumor on David's liver.

David also has three or four small lumps on his lungs, three on his left and possibly one on his right. These lumps are what the doctors will be looking at first because they are easiest and safest to get to. We'll schedule this biopsy sometime next week. The pathologists will examine the tissue to see if it is anything to worry about.

The surgeon said it is possible that the lumps on his lungs could be some kind of fungal infection that is fairly common in this area. It is also possible that the lumps are cancerous tumors, either a totally separate cancer or a spreading of the cancer from his liver.

If it is just an infection (or some other kind of nothing-special goop) the surgeons will go ahead and do a biopsy of the adrenal gland growth. If the lung lumps are cancerous they won't bother checking out the adrenal gland (or at least, not in a big hurry) because they'll already know to rule out a transplant.

We asked why the doctors couldn't do a biopsy of both the lungs and the gland tissue at the same time, thinking that we'd get answers on both and he'd only have one anesthesia to deal with. Taking tissue from the lung isn't as invasive or dangerous as taking tissue from the abdomen. Why expose David to the risk of surgery on his abdomen when, if the lung tissue is cancerous, we already have the answers we need?

These last few days have been very strange. I'm sure people wondered why I went back to work for a couple of days. I guess I have to have at least a little bit of "normal" in my life right now. Having something important to do (my students are very important to me) gives me something to focus on, something positive I can pour my energy into while diverting my mind from the unthinkable.

Recently, I was struck by how easy it was to "forget" about what's happening with David for a while. I was also struck by how hard it was to keep my focus, my composure; heck, even my sanity during those times when I was forced to remember. Those "remember" moments came out of nowhere and hit me like a hammer. I'd have to take a few minutes to catch my breath before I could refocus on what I was supposed to be doing.

I thought this was supposed to get easier.

The End

April 20, 2008, 10:05 p.m.

We made it down to St. Louis this afternoon. It's going to be a long trip, especially tomorrow as we wait for David to get out of biopsy surgery. It will also seem like forever until we get results. We hope we'll have everything we need before we come home this weekend.

It's strange. As bad as I've felt about things lately and as dark as I've been when I think about how things could turn out, I actually feel hopeful today. This is the first time in several days that I've felt like things will be okay.

I'm not going into this with blinders on, and I'm not going to be completely blindsided and unprepared if things turn out badly, but I can feel a budding of hope within me again. When I smile it isn't forced and that's a great feeling, made better by how rare it's been lately.

David will get his biopsy early tomorrow and will spend at least the remainder of the day in the intensive care unit. We hope that he'll spend tomorrow night in a regular patient room on the ninth floor so we can all be a little more comfortable. We're not sure just yet where we'll be if he has to spend the night in intensive care. Perhaps the hospital will open up the room that he'll have Tuesday for us late on Monday – once they are certain they won't have to use the room for someone else. We could at least have someplace where we could rest a bit and maybe take a shower.

April 21, 2008, 10:18 a.m.

This day is just flying by. David went in to surgery at about 9 a.m. and he just came out a few minutes ago. The surgeon told us that things went very well and that he was able to find the spots easily by sticking a scope in through a small cut in his chest. They were even able to remove the tumor using that same incision. That's good news. Before the surgery, they told us that they might have to make a much larger incision in David's chest if they had a hard time finding the tumor or if it was in a spot where it wasn't easy to remove.

He's in the recovery room right now waking up. They won't let us see him until he's a bit more conscious, so I wanted to steal a few minutes to update everyone. He'll have a drainage tube in his chest for a day or two and that might be a bit irritating, maybe even painful, but nowhere near as bad as it would have been if the surgeons had been forced to make a three- or four-inch hole in David's side.

Once David is finished in the recovery room, we'll take him to the intensive care unit where we'll finally be able to feed him. He hasn't had anything to eat or drink since about 10:30 last night. Because of a stupid tradition (superstition? stupidstition?) that I've maintained since our first visit I also have not had anything to eat since that time last night. Rachel had an omelet and some granola this morning, but who's keeping track?

We're still hoping that this lump turns out to be benign. If it is then we can schedule a biopsy of David's adrenal gland in about two weeks. Both biopsies have to come back benign before the doctors will okay a liver transplant.

Rachel and I are both still feeling hopeful about today and the rest of this week. I've got a good feeling about our situation for the first time in what feels like a very long time. In reality, it's probably only been about a week that I've been down about things, but a week wondering if your son is going to live or die and knowing that there's nothing you can do to influence the outcome is one helluva long week. Trust me. I don't recommend the experience to anyone.

April 21, 2008, 3:49 p.m.

David is awake - awake and hungry! He's still pretty sore, but he receives morphine every hour so his pain is manageable. He seems to be recovering quickly and it is quite possible that we will be moved out of the PICU [*Pediatric Intensive Care Unit*] and into a regular hospital room tonight. The nurses told us that it is pretty standard procedure to house children his age in the unit after most types of surgery – just in case. I guess older kids can tell the doctors when things don't feel right, thus indicating potential problems, but babies can't do that yet.

Overall, he looks good all things considered. He's got a big tangle of tubes and wires coming out of and off of him so he looks kind of like Frankenbaby. Those tubes and wires look worse than they really are. Only one or two of them are actually imbedded, a drainage tube from his right lung and the tube from his chest. The rest are all leads and sensors that keep track of his vital signs.

Even with all this mess of equipment on him, he managed a quick smile. Rachel's parents joined us today. It's great having family that lives close to the hospital. That little extra bit of support, and a grin or two from David, make a big difference. It might have been a combination of the morphine and his first bottle of the day, but I like to think it was because he was feeling better and because his grandpa was making faces at him.

The surgeon told us that we probably won't know the results of the surgery, benign or malignant, for a few days. We had hoped the doctors could take a frozen pathology section (I'm not quite sure exactly what that means) that would tell us either yes or no for cancer, but the tumor was too small for that.

It is possible that we'll have results before we come home, but it is equally possible that we'll have to make another drive down here next week for the results. That's one frustration I have with this process. Nobody wants to tell us anything over the phone. It doesn't seem to matter to them that we have a three and a half hour drive just to talk to them for 20 minutes. I guess they paid all that money for those bedside manner classes and they want to get the chance to use those skills face-to-face.

April 22, 2008, 11:11 a.m.

We've been held hostage in the PICU almost all morning. I didn't realize that, when doctors start their rounds at 7:30 a.m., no one is allowed in or out of the unit until they are finished - in this case about 10:45 a.m. This includes restroom breaks. OUCH!

There's a neat little space-shuttle/submarine toilet in each of the PICU rooms that folds out from underneath the sink, but I cannot imagine using that unless I'm in dire need. Everything is on display in those little glass boxes they call patient rooms. Don't get me wrong. I'm glad that the rooms are easily watched and accessible in case there are medical problems for the patient, it's just a little inconvenient now and then.

David is doing well (lucky kid … diapers!) and we expect to be moved to the ninth floor sometime soon. The doctors have scheduled another x-ray to check on the placement of the drainage tube and to make sure fluids are actually draining from his lungs like they should be. Everything was fine when the doctors checked him over this morning, so we don't expect any complications. We should be in the new room (with a private bathroom - yay!) by early- to mid-afternoon.

We'll all be together tonight, which will be nice. Last night, Rachel stayed in the PICU. I slept on a chair in the family waiting room and made frequent visits to check on things. Don't worry about me though. I wasn't lonely. The room was packed with people, many of whom snored just like Rachel so I felt right at home.

(Yeah, I know that was a cheap shot and I'm gonna get it when Rachel reads this … but I couldn't help myself. Hehehe!)

David's spirits have been high but then, thanks to the morphine, so has David. We even managed to make him smile and laugh a bit last night before he went to bed. That was a great relief. The only time he seems like he is in pain today is when he coughs. The doctors said the drainage tube pushes directly against his right lung, so sudden intakes or exhalations of breath can really hurt.

It's strange. I've said several times that David reminds me of my grandfather and this is just another reminder. When Don was in the hospital having part of his lung removed because of lung cancer the only time he seemed to be in pain was when he coughed. The resemblance between the two is uncanny, especially when one considers how David has a wave in the little bit of hair he has left that looks a little like grandpas.

April 22, 2008, 8:03 p.m.

David's drainage tube should come out tonight. That means all of us should get a better night's sleep tonight and we might all be able to come home soon. I'm not going to count on that, but it is nice to hear. Remember, we thought for a while that our first big stay here would be about three or four days, five or six on the outside. We were here for something like 12 days.

Yeah, the two stays are completely different but I don't want to get my hopes up over something like this. I'll save my hope for something important – like the results of this stay.

David is feeling well and has spent a lot more time awake today than he did yesterday. He still has some pain and still gets regular morphine, but he is handling things a little better. He has a slight fever that is a little troublesome, but so far nobody has made a big deal about it so I'm not going to worry.

I don't know what it is about this place. Maybe it is the decor or the specialty areas – like the garden, the school, the play rooms, etc. – or maybe it is the people we meet here, staff and patients alike, but there is something very life affirming about St. Louis Children's Hospital. I find it hard to be here and not have some extra measure of hope for David's future.

This is not to say that our local hospital isn't a hopeful place. Certainly the people there are amazing and have always treated us with the utmost care and professionalism. We've become very close with some of the nurses. If it wasn't for the fact that seeing them means David is in the hospital for something unpleasant, we are always happy to see them.

Still, there is just something about SLCH that makes me feel like things are going to be OK. I know that I'm not the only person who feels this way. The other parents I've talked to here, even those whose children are in serious trouble, have nothing but positive things to say about this hospital. They all say that they appreciate the positive nature of this hospital and how they are treated like people, not patients.

April 23, 2008, 6:34 p.m.

David's cancer has spread to his lungs. The doctors said they cannot give us the transplant we've been waiting for and that David probably has about a year to live.

We need to be alone with this news for a while.

April 24, 2008, 10:54 a.m.

David still plays with his toys and enjoys throwing them to the floor to see if we'll pick them up for him. He giggles and rubs his chest when he hears me shaking his bottle. He wants his daddy to tickle him when he's feeling playful and he wants his mother to hold him when he's feeling cranky.

And in a year from now he might not be here anymore.

I'm still stunned and hollow inside from the news we received yesterday. Nothing quite feels real.

I know that doctors are not always right and that miracles can happen. Everyone has heard a story about people with seemingly hopeless cancers suddenly going into remission and live long and healthy lives. Certainly that kind of thing can happen here, but I'm not going to pin all of my hopes on a "maybe" or a "could be." I have to be prepared for what will most likely happen.

The most likely course of events is that we will start a new regimen of chemotherapy in the very near future. We'll give David whatever fighting chance we can, even going so far as to apply for experimental treatments. Ultimately, however, this precious baby boy is probably going to die within about a year.

We know that God answers every prayer, but that sometimes the answer is "No."

Where we used to hear things like "recovery options" and "transplant procedures," we're now hearing about "quality of life" issues and how we can make the most of whatever time we have left.

Rachel and I have talked about this quite a bit since Wednesday evening and we've made a decision. We're not going to watch our son die. We're going to watch our son live! We are not going to waste our time crying and feeling sorry for ourselves. David's Godmother used a phrase one time about how we're going to have to be like Tigger from Winnie the Pooh and just kept bouncing, 'cause that's what Tiggers do best! We're going to enjoy being Tiggers and we're not going to let cancer destroy us.

Sure, realistically we're going to have some pretty dark days ahead of us, but we are going to do our best to stay positive. For that, we're going to need help. We want people to smile when they see David. We want him to know that he's surrounded by happy people who love him and are glad to see him.

We will need help to stay positive. There are going to be times when we want to talk about David's cancer but most of the time we will want to talk about normal, everyday life. We know what David's up against, but that's not the only thing happening in the world. We certainly don't want to focus only on cancer because that would be to deny that there are other things in life.

If you used to talk to us about politics, then know that we're still interested in that. If you talked to us about movies, then know that we still want to watch movies. If you used to talk to us about the great game you watched on ESPN last night, then you probably didn't know us very well. We both hate sports.

We should be coming home either late this afternoon or mid-day tomorrow. We should be up to having a few visitors Saturday or

Sunday.

As always, thank you for your thoughts, your prayers and your positive energy. We need it now more than ever.

April 27, 2008 10:32 p.m.

I was reminded again tonight about how great it is to have friends and family for support during times of trouble. I don't know if I can describe how special is it to have people around who don't think they are doing anything special by being around.

I was also given a great piece of advice today that I'd recommend for anyone, but especially for people who are going through some kind of crisis. Check out *The Last Lecture* by Randy Pausch. He speaks for himself so I'm not going to bother trying to introduce him or his work.

April 29, 2008, 9:02 p.m.

My son is dying.

We went to St. Louis Children's Hospital this morning to have a consultation with David's doctor. She confirmed yet again that David's cancer has spread from his liver to his lungs and his adrenal gland. She also confirmed that he probably has about a year to live.

Most of our conversation revolved around options for future treatment. Ultimately, we decided that David would begin using an experimental treatment that has been shown to slow the progress of metastatic disease (aggressive cancers). He will begin this process in June because he has to be at least a year old before he can be a part of this study.

This drug will not save David's life. The most it will do is perhaps prolong his life a short while without too many nasty side effects. The side effects from this drug will be similar to those of the chemotherapy he has already undergone but without the hair loss (we hope).

The preliminary work (scans, blood-work, etc.) will likely begin a few weeks before he starts the new medicine because the doctors in the study have to have a baseline by which to judge the drug's effectiveness.

The other options that were presented to us were not very good in our opinion.

The first option was to do nothing. David's cancer would progress normally until it killed him. He wouldn't have a very long life, but the life he had would be relatively pain free until he really went downhill. That downhill period could have been as little as a day or as long as several weeks.

The second option was to use different medicine, including several drugs that he would have to take two or three times each day. He would be constantly fatigued, irritable and in quite a bit of pain, but his life would probably be prolonged by a few months. We didn't think the extra time was worth the cost of seeing him deteriorate slowly. I don't know how I could handle that.

We went with the option that gave us a possibility for extending David's life while still giving him the best quality of life.

I'm sure there are people reading this right now that are

shocked or offended that we wouldn't go with the option that gave us the most possible time. All I can say is that I'm sorry you feel that way and request that you keep your opinion to yourself. I hope you never find yourself in a situation where you have to make this kind of choice.

Please respect us enough to know that, even if you disagree, we did the best we could with a difficult decision. I am certain that I will be haunted by the necessity to make this decision and I'll be second-guessing myself for the rest of my life. Please know that expressing doubts about our decision will only make a bad situation worse.

Before anyone asks, we have more than one doctor's opinion on this. The hemoc [*hematology-oncology*] team at SLCH agrees that the options presented to us were the only options with a chance of success. Surgery to remove the tumor was regarded as unfeasible. Our SLCH doctor also sent David's entire file to a doctor in Washington, D.C. who is the nation's foremost expert in rhabdoid tumors and he agreed that the three options we were given were the best.

We'll be checking in with our doctor here in Champaign to be sure he concurs but we're fairly certain that he won't have anything to add.

May 2, 2008, 6:18 p.m.

David was in the emergency room last night for a fever – 101 degrees. It was just enough of a temperature for us to call the doctors, but not enough to really worry.

When this whole thing started, the doctors warned us that we should call for any fever above 100 degrees because it could be a sign of an infection. With his chest tube in place any infection could be very serious. After all, the tube runs almost directly into his heart - certainly nothing to play around with.

It turned out that David's fever was probably just because of teething or possibly a slight cold. Whew! We caught a break. They took a blood culture (just to be sure), gave him an antibiotic and did their best to make him laugh. I think the laughing helped most of all because he'd been cranky. We made it home after a couple of hours.

Even with all that going on I was still able to do something that I've been thinking about ever since we learned David's long-term prognosis last week. I got my first tattoo. It's an honorific/memorial for David. It features the DC Comics logo. I'm a nerd and those are his initials. It also has his birthday and the Latin phrase *Vivo Fidens Postremo*, which roughly translates to "Live Without Fear From Now On." It's not pretty. I don't mean the tattoo. That's actually pretty cool. I'm warning you that the arm on which the tattoo was placed is rather pale and a little flabby.

Man, I have to hit the gym! I look kinda like a melted candle, all saggy and just a little wrong.

May 6, 2008, 6:56 p.m.

We had a situation today. I'm still not sure what the end result will be so I can't say if it is a bad situation or not.

David had a blood draw yesterday, a regularly scheduled thing

87

we do every Monday and Thursday. It turned out his hemoglobin was a bit low. We scheduled a transfusion for late this morning - no big rush but we needed to get it done.

The scare came once David was admitted and they started doing the pre-transfusion checks. He had a fever with temperatures between 101 and 102 degrees on and off. They gave him some medication and settled in to wait for his temperature to come down because they try not to give transfusions to patients with fevers.

By late afternoon the fever still hadn't gone away so the doctors and nurses started to worry that he might have some kind of an infection, possibly in or around his chest tube.

That's when I got the call on my cell phone that something could be wrong. I was in the middle of a staff meeting at school, and I just bolted. I had to get to the hospital.

Nothing could go wrong if I'm there, right?!?

It was gratifying to see that several people left the meeting and took off running right behind me – almost as if their own children were the ones in trouble. Their only questions were, "What's wrong?" and "How can I help?" I know that the meeting could very well have cleared out if that's what I needed. (I also know that family members, both near and far, would be here as soon as they could if that's what we needed, but the friends from school are the ones I saw today so they are the ones getting special mention here.)

Have I mentioned recently how good it is to have friends who show that kind of support? I don't know how I could get through this if I didn't know that these people have my back.

Funny Side Note: The student I wrote about earlier, the one I tricked when I tested the transplant beeper, was in the hall outside the staff meeting when I got the call from Rachel this afternoon. She saw the look on my face and watched me running. She probably thought, "Oh no, I'm not falling for that again!"

It turned out that blood cultures taken from the chest tube were fine and the tube was clear. Whew, good news.

But wait ...

David's hemoglobin kept on dropping and his fever didn't go away. The nurses did another blood culture and the results came back that his hemoglobin was 4-point-something. I guess the restriction on giving transfusions to patients with fevers doesn't come into play when the numbers are this low because they quickly hooked him up.

Our Champaign doctor came in to talk to us a bit ago. He said he doesn't think there is any kind of internal bleeding that could be causing these low numbers. David would be in a lot more pain and he'd show signs of abdominal cramps (pulling his legs in tight, tenderness on his stomach, etc.) if he was bleeding.

Another option is that his rhabdoid tumor is starting to affect David's bone marrow and causing it to slow down blood production. If today's transfusion doesn't help out and blood production doesn't pick up by Thursday's blood draw we may have to schedule a bone marrow biopsy to see what's happening there.

Yet another possibility is that everything that David's had going on lately (cancer in at least two spots, several hospital visits, teething, colds, mysterious fevers, jet-lag, hangovers, and Lotto mania - okay, not those last few) could have just caught up with him and knocked his system for a loop.

Rachel's been a real trooper today. She's been with him in the hospital all day and she'll stay over tonight but even she has her limits. She hasn't cried but she keeps saying, "I'm not ready yet. I'm not ready to lose him yet" I don't know what I can say to make her feel better or how to reassure her.

I'm not ready yet either.

May 8, 2008, 5:45 a.m.

I started making funeral arrangements for my son yesterday.

David's in some sporadic pain so he's only sleeping in spurts. It's about 5:30 a.m. and I keep thinking that I made funeral arrangements yesterday. I even had to sign the paperwork saying what we wanted the doctors to do when David's heart stops. It doesn't seem possible and it certainly isn't right. This isn't the way it is supposed to work.

Parents aren't supposed to think about burying their children. We're supposed to worry about getting their immunizations on time or whether they are getting their homework done. We're supposed to worry about how we're going to pay for college, if he'll get into a good school, and whether he'll major in something flighty, like theater (right Mom?).

We're supposed to worry about whether or not we have enough life insurance, not whether he has enough. He's not even a year old. I shouldn't have to wonder if now is the right time to start writing his obituary because I know I'll have to write one sooner or later and it will be really hard to do it later.

Damn it! It's not supposed to be like this.

David received a second unit of blood two nights ago because his hemoglobin stayed low so he stayed in the hospital for a few days.

I went to school yesterday because it was only a half day and I didn't think anything important was going to happen at the hospital. David has had transfusions before and he's always come out of them smiling and feeling lively and full of energy. I remember a few years ago, there was a big scandal because athletes were giving themselves transfusions before big events because they felt, and performed better, with the extra blood.

I got the call to come back to the hospital at around 9 or 9:30 a.m. Something was wrong. I hope I didn't scare too many of my students. They know that when they see a fat guy running something serious is going on. Well, I was running.

The doctors said the tumor in David's liver seemed to be growing quickly and that David was likely bleeding into it (thus the low hemoglobin counts). We could see a slightly raised lump on his right side. They did a CT scan that showed some confusing results. There was some bleeding but not enough to account for all of the low blood numbers. The doctors seem legitimately stumped. Where did all of that blood from the first transfusion go? They still don't know.

Regardless, he is still bleeding. It's just slower than they originally thought it would be. It is possible that the bleeding will stop on its own for a while, but it will most likely continue being a "slow bleed" which would mean that David could live for a little while longer, perhaps even a few weeks. We're looking into hospice care to help keep David comfortable at home.

David's "slow bleed" could also easily become a "quick bleed" which would mean that David's life would be measured in hours, perhaps as long as a day if we are lucky. There isn't anything doctors can do.

It's odd to think that this could be a blessing. Last week, when we thought David still had about a year to live, we told our doctors that we did not want David to have a drawn-out, painful battle that he would end up losing eventually anyway. We wanted something that was going to be quick and easier for him.

We thought we'd have a year. We were wrong.

It's not supposed to be this way.

May 8, 2008, 2:33 p.m.

David is coming home today.

We're setting up a hospice care program that will keep him as pain free as possible for the time he has left. He'll probably be sleeping a lot, but at least he'll be sleeping in his own bed.

Our doctors gave us the latest news this morning. Given everything they saw on the CT scans and things, they've learned from blood tests and simple observation, they believe David's cancer may have spread to his bones and possibly into his brain. The bone cancer would explain why his blood counts have been odd, and it would also explain the pain David's been experiencing.

The only thing we can do now is modify his pain medication and make him comfortable. Further tests, such as a bone marrow biopsy, would be very painful and it wouldn't help anything. Sure, we'd know whether or not David has cancer in his bones but that knowledge wouldn't do us any good. The prognosis wouldn't change.

The best we can hope for right now is that David will live relatively comfortably and pain free for about three weeks. It is possible that we have even less time than that.

I've put in word with the doctors at St. Louis Children's Hospital and Washington University that we'll allow them to examine David's body when he's done with it. They have been studying him throughout this process to see what they can learn about treating this rare form of cancer.

While the thought of someone performing an autopsy on my beautiful boy is very upsetting, it is something we have to do. Perhaps the doctors will use what they learn from studying David to find a way to treat or even cure this disease and save other families from going through this pain. I don't know if I could live with myself if I didn't at least let them try.

Also, we've let the doctors here and in St. Louis know that we want them to use any part of him they can use as transplant material. We understand that most of David's organs are corrupt and that they won't be able to use much, but maybe his corneas can help a blind kid see again or his skin can help a burn victim or a tendon might help a child walk. We don't want to cheat those babies of their opportunities to live the life we wanted David to have.

I wrote an obituary today. I'm talking with the people at the funeral home tomorrow morning. All of this still feels unreal. Is that one of the stages of grief? I'm not in denial (at least I don't think I am in denial … am I denying denial?). I know what's going on, and I've all but given up the bargaining stage but I'm not quite ready for acceptance.

I wonder if I'll ever be ready.

May 10, 2008, 11:43 p.m.

You know what? In times like these, not even Southern Comfort is all that comforting.

May 11, 2008, 10:38 a.m.

Mother's Day.

This is our first Mother's Day since having David and the only one Rachel is going to have with him. Mother's Day is a very special holiday for our family because it was this day two years ago that Rachel and I decided that we would start trying to have a child. She'd wanted one for quite a while and I had been hesitant. Her "Mother's Day gift" from me that year was agreeing that she should be a mother.

Last year I gave Rachel a present even though she was still pregnant, and not technically a mother yet. Actually, I set her up. I told her that she wasn't my mother, so I wasn't going to give her anything. That was just to keep the element of surprise. Actually, I gave her about $350 worth of gift cards to all of her favorite clothing stores, $25 or $50 to each store. The idea was that once David was born she could go on a guilt-free shopping spree with her friends to celebrate the fact that she wasn't in maternity clothes anymore. All of our friends joked and said that I was setting the bar too high and that I'd have to beat that mark this year.

For Father's Day last year I had the best possible present. I got David. He was born on June 15, just before Father's Day. He was still in the hospital when Father's Day rolled around because he was premature. He was doing well, but his bilirubin numbers were a little high and he was a bit jaundiced (side note: That Billy Ruben guy must have been one yellow dude if they named the jaundice scale after him).

I remember stopping in the drug store so I could buy my father-in-law a Father's Day card. I stood in that aisle weeping like a child because I was so happy and proud.

This year Rachel and I decided that we aren't going to do anything special for Mother's Day or, if David lasts that long, Father's Day. Instead we're going to save any money we would have spent and hold a party for David next summer, kind of like a wake, but happier.

We want to remember him and honor him in an appropriate way, with smiles.

May 14, 2008 8:36 a.m.

I crossed off another item on my "Daddy's To Do List" yesterday.

I took David to Miller Park Zoo in Bloomington [*Illinois*]. I've always had a special connection with that zoo because my father used to take me there several times a year when I was a boy. I performed in community theater at that park the summer Rachel and I got engaged. I even mentioned our engagement in the play's program book. I wanted to add David to my list of happy memories associated with the park.

David loved being there. It was a combination of several things (being outside, seeing the animals, lots of children running around and time with Dad) that made him smile almost all day. It's strange, with all of the exotic tigers, leopards, gibbons, etc. that they have at Miller Park, the one animal David liked the most was the chicken.

A CHICKEN!?!

David loved watching a black chicken strut around the petting zoo area. He'd reach out his hands toward the fence as if he wanted to pet it and then he'd turn back around to look at me with a big, cheesy, three-toothed grin on his face. The petting area was closed while we were there or David would have been all over that bird like, well, like me on a fried version of that bird.

We toured the rainforest area and the big animal house. We even watched the otter playing (my favorite) but nothing made David's face light up more than the chicken. I guess all of the animals were exotic to David but I wish I could tell a more macho version of this story … "Yeah, my kid loved it when the tiger roared. That didn't scare him a bit." Or, "I swear, he tried to beat his chest just like the ape. It was awesome!"

Nope, I get the chicken story.

We took a walk around the pond while David was feeling a little sleepy and we rode the carousel when he was ready for some fun. Overall, it was a great trip to the zoo.

At one point, however, I started to take a turn into dark territory. I'm not going to let this taint my memory of David at the zoo, but it was a little rough.

A woman with a baby a little older than David walked by and the two children locked eyes. Other than the chicken, I'd have to say that this little girl was what held his attention the most. We talked for a few minutes, exchanging pleasantries about how much our children were enjoying themselves and which exhibits they liked the most (a chicken … for cryin' out loud!).

Eventually the woman asked how old David was and, after I told her that he was almost 11 months, she leaned in close to him, smiled broadly, and commented on how we must be really looking forward to his first birthday party.

I died a little bit right then.

My mouth went dry, and my voice caught in my throat. I think my eyes probably misted up a bit. I didn't have the heart to tell her the truth. I couldn't tell her that he probably won't have a first birthday party. I didn't want her to feel bad for saying the wrong thing when she couldn't have known better, so I just smiled weakly and said, "I hope so."

May 17, 2008, 7:31 p.m.

I just got back from taking a few laps at the Champaign County
Relay for Life. For people who don't know, the event is a fundraiser
awareness-raiser for cancer and cancer research. It's a great event
that celebrates life, encourages those struggling to survive, and
honors those who have died.

The event kicks off with a survivor lap. Anyone who is
fighting cancer or who has beaten cancer is invited to take a lap
around the high school track. Everyone else at the event lines the
track and packs the stands to give survivors a standing ovation. It is
incredible.

I've been involved in the Relay for Life for several years,
usually walking on company teams. I've even walked in some events
as a stand-in for people who I knew and loved, such as my mother
and grandfather, who were either survivors or who had lost their
battle.

This is the first year I was invited to join the survivor lap
carrying David, of course.

That was the longest, hardest lap I've ever had to walk. I kept
thinking about how next year, instead of walking with David in my
arms, I'll be walking in David's memory. I'll be carrying a picture of
my son instead of carrying him. I'm still having a hard time
reconciling myself to the fact that he's going to be gone within a few
weeks. It doesn't seem possible, but it's going to happen.

For me, one of the best things about the Relay is the luminaries. Each year, as donations are made, cancer survivors' and cancer victims' names are added to white paper bags. Volunteers put candles in the bags and then light them up at dusk for a beautiful display surrounding the track.

I saw David's name on several bags this year. During one of my laps I stopped at each luminary bearing his name. I took a few moments to think about how he had touched the lives of the people who bought the luminaries in his name.

I was deeply touched to see several of my students' names as donors.

Earlier today, as sort of a precursor to the Relay, we took David to my mother's house for a family get-together. Both sides of the family mine and Rachel's, spent several hours together. Both sets of grandparents, aunts, and cousins were together for the first time since Rachel and I got married.

The family reunion was nice but, like the Relay for Life, there was a bit of bitter-sweet downside. For some of the family members present, it could be the last time they see David alive.

Today was supposed to be a celebration of life, and in many ways it has been. It was great to see so many people, both at the Relay for Life and at the family get together, that care about the survivors and who are sending out prayers, good thoughts and positive energy. Still, for us, there is always a 600 pound gorilla in the room. In a few weeks, the world is going to be a little darker.

Until that day, I'm going to stand in David's light for as long as possible.

May 21, 2008, 11:26 p.m.

It's kind of strange tonight. In half an hour, David will have surpassed our most recent worst-case-scenario. As of tomorrow, it will have been two weeks since our doctors said David had two or three weeks to live.

Could it be that my son has only one week left? It doesn't seem possible (there's that denial thing coming in again). He has had a rough couple of days. Lots of sleeping and he hasn't wanted to eat much. We attributed that to his pain medication more than anything else. We switched things up a bit today, and he seemed much better. He was hungrier than he's been in several days and he was a bit more aware of what's going on around him.

Still, I cannot deny what's happening. He's dying and I have to watch it happen.

David's liver tumor has grown large enough that we can see the hard ridge of tissue through his shirts. He hardly ever wakes up for more than a few minutes at a time and in the past three days he's eaten about as much as he would have eaten in an afternoon two months ago.

I confirmed some of the arrangements with the funeral home today and I made plans with our parish priests to have David receive the sacrament of last rites soon. I know I keep saying this, but it was a surreal experience. It was almost like it was happening to someone else and I was just watching it on television. It didn't feel real until I had to tell Rachel what I'd done with my afternoon. Trust me, that's not an easy conversation to have.

Knowing how soon an end could come for David, Rachel and I have redoubled our efforts to make these last few days special. We both took David to Miller Park Zoo yesterday. He was so out of it during the trip that not even the chickens could get much of a reaction out of David (don't get me started again on those FRICKIN' CHICKENS!).

I joke about the chickens, but before anyone calls foul (get it ... fowl ... I crack myself up), I want people to know that the Weber family officially adopted the Miller Park Zoo's Japanese Silky Chicken in David's name. We'll get a certificate in the mail soon and the zoo will hang a copy of the certificate in the entryway for a brief time. I'm not going to say how much it cost. Suffice to say it wasn't chicken feed (Ooohhh! I did it again!).

We ended the day by taking David on a tour of the Illinois State University campus. We showed him where his parents met for the first time in Basic Acting class, Centennial West room 30, and the so-called Airport Lounge where we hung out. Non-ISU theater types should just imagine a scene from a romantic college movie where people drink coffee and pretentiously discuss plays they've only half-read/half-understood, and you'll get the picture of what those days were like for us.

We also took David to meet his grandfather, sort of.

My dad died when I was about twelve so there really isn't any way for David to meet him. We did the next best thing & took David on a tour of Illinois State University's TV-10 news studio. Dad was one of the two professors at ISU who started the campus TV station. The studio was dedicated to his memory a few years ago. I cannot think of any place on earth where my father's spirit can be more vividly felt than there.

We took some pictures of David by the TV-10 sign and others of him holding Dad's picture. We probably shouldn't have pulled it off the wall but we didn't really care at the time. Honestly, what would they do, scream at us for putting a dead grandpa's picture into the hands of a dying baby? Hardly!

(Okay, that last bit was a little harsh but it's been a long day and I'm entitled to a little cynicism now and then.)

Overall, it was one of the best days we've had in a long time. Future plans include going for a hike and maybe camping out in a tent in our backyard – things all fathers should have on their Daddy-To-Do lists and things I'm not going to let cancer cheat me out of.

I wish I would have the opportunity to do other things on my list: teach him to fish, play catch, drive a car, etc. but I'm going to do everything I can while I still have him. Sure, it's probably a bit greedy of me and I know he isn't going to know the difference, but I don't care. I want to get as much "Dad Time" as I can.

May 25, 2008, 1:43 p.m.

Yesterday was a great day. David started out by going to daycare to play with the other kids. He seemed to enjoy that even though he slept quite a bit.

For me, though, the highlight of the day came when we headed over to Lake of the Woods for a hike. I had David strapped to my chest in a carrier, kind of like a backpack that holds babies. We stayed on trails that were fairly flat and even so that there was very little chance of falling. David loves being outside lately so he had a good time.

Since we've changed his medication David has been much more aware of his surroundings but still doesn't seem to be in any pain. He will make eye contact, occasionally, and he will reach out for things he wants like his toys, his bottle or someone to hold him. It's nice to see that he is still "with it" enough to let us know how he's doing.

It's hard to believe that we are closing in on the end. According to the prognosis, David has four days left. I know these predictions are not always accurate and that he could have quite a bit more time than the original estimate. Still, I wonder about whether he'll make it to his first birthday. If he does we are planning to have some kind of party. It will probably be something small, just a few friends and a cake decorated like a chicken.

Rachel is taking some much-needed time off today. I arranged for her to have a surprise. I scheduled manicures & pedicures for her and three of her friends then, once they get back home, I have chocolate-covered strawberries and strawberry margaritas for them to enjoy. She needed this break and it makes me feel good to do something nice for her. It gave me something positive to focus on for a while as I was setting things up, something good to anticipate for a change.

May 26, 2008, 8:37 p.m.

All day I've been thinking about something that happened to me yesterday.

I went to the grocery store to buy a few things we needed around the house, including a can of formula for David. He hasn't been eating much in the past week or so. He usually eats a bit of yogurt and drinks a bit of formula, but the amounts are startling. In an average day he will eat about as much as he would eat in a single sitting a month ago.

He's losing a lot of weight, but he doesn't seem hungry. Our hospice nurse said we shouldn't think of him as starving himself. He isn't feeling hungry. Instead, we should think of this as the cancer running its course.

As I was picking up the can of formula I actually had this thought, "I should only get the half-sized can. He probably won't live long enough to need the full-sized can. I wouldn't want to waste it." I was immediately ashamed of myself for thinking such a callous thought. Still, the reality of our situation is such that I probably was right. I lose him a little bit more every day.

I pulled myself together and managed to keep from choking up in the grocery store. I'm glad that I didn't see anybody I know. My facade wouldn't have stood up to any kind of scrutiny. I had to drive around the neighborhood for a little while before I felt confident enough to go home.

Even though I've been thinking about that incident all day, we have managed to have a pretty good Memorial Day. It is starting to sound like a cliché but I marked off another item from my "Daddy-To-Do" list this evening. I shared a beer with my son.

Okay, I need to explain before people start calling the Department of Children and Family Services. I did not put a nipple on a Corona bottle and pass it over to my son. We were cooking out this evening in celebration of Memorial Day. I opened up a beer and walked around the backyard holding the bottle in one hand and my son in the other. We had a few moments to talk father-to-son, something my father and I used to do when I was a kid.

As I walked around in the yard I pointed out where he would have played this summer. I told him how I imagined what he would look like as a toddler. I said I saw him running around that yard, falling occasionally but always laughing, as his daddy chased him. I showed him where I had imagined him jumping into a pile of leaves this fall or building a snow fort this winter like I built with my father in one of the proudest son-father moments of my childhood. I showed him where I would have liked to put a little swing set, slide or castle/playhouse where he could play with his friends.

I guess I had a memorial on Memorial Day for someone who wasn't gone yet. I remembered things that were very real in my mind even though they hadn't happened yet. It may sound sad, but it was a great day for me.

Today I saw David's childhood as it should have been.

May 29, 2008, 8:37 a.m.

So, this is what borrowed time feels like ...

This is D-Day for us. This afternoon marks three weeks since the doctors told us we could expect David to live for two or three more weeks. He's lost a lot of weight, he is really weak, and he sleeps a lot because of his pain medication, but he's still with us and still occasionally responding to us.

We never know exactly what's going to get a reaction from him. Sometimes it is a certain person holding him or a voice he recognizes, other times it is a special toy that he wants to hold (usually one of his plastic rings). Sometimes it can be a formula bottle, yogurt, or ice cream that he wants and still other times he'll be fascinated by something completely unpredictable (like a chicken?!?). We're grateful for any and all of those things because they show us that our son is still with us. I cannot fool myself into believing that these precious moments of recognition mean he's going to recover. I can tell that an end is coming soon and that this is just a temporary reprieve.

I'm going to try to focus my energy today on things that will bring my mood up. I'm going to pay extra attention to my son today and be thankful for all of the wonderful support we've been given throughout this ordeal.

The friends, family, and neighbors who have offered a kind word, a pat on the shoulder or an understanding look have been a Godsend for us. Co-workers, the PTA, the Gopher Guys*, the owners of Skateland Skating Rink, and hundreds of others (including

106

many virtual strangers who have offered love and support) have come out to offer us the right kind of hope, hope that there really is a light in all of this darkness.

*[The Gopher Guys are Dave and Heather Hoover and the rest of the people who frequent Armored Gopher Games in Urbana, IL, nerd friends who rallied around us even though they barely knew us at the time. They started a fund drive among their customers just because they heard a fellow gamer was in trouble. That kind of support from out of the blue was heartening, healing, and faith restoring.]

That light is there, even if we can't always see it.

May 30, 2008, 10:16 a.m.

David is gone.

He died at 10:40 p.m. last night. I was holding him when it happened and Rachel was next to him holding his hand.

His breathing started getting ragged a little before 7 p.m. and by 7:30 our hospice nurse was on her way. We held him and tried to talk to him about happy memories we have; hearing him cry for the first time in the delivery room and seeing him laugh out loud for the first time are two of the memories that stick out most clearly in my mind. We tried hard not to cry and sob because we didn't want his last moments to be surrounded by sadness. We wanted him to hear us laughing and telling him how much we loved him and how proud we were of him.

I still cannot believe that I won't be able to hold him anymore or that I won't get to watch him destroy his first birthday cake. I won't hear him laugh any more or see him rub his belly when he is really thrilled and excited by something.

Our hospice nurse was fantastic. She stayed with us the entire time – up until the directors came out to take us to the funeral home. She was there with a bit of advice or support when we needed her, but she was unobtrusive when we needed privacy.

People have said that Rachel and I have shown a lot of strength and courage during this time. I disagree. We have only done what we've had to do. We didn't have a choice. The people who have shown us real strength are the hospice workers, the critical care nurses, and the other people who have helped us during these past few months. They could have worked in any kind of nursing but they made a choice. They opted to help people through the last days of their lives. They have real strength and courage because they have had other options but they still chose to help people who need it.

I know I am going to remember those last few minutes with David for the rest of my life. Still, I'm going to try to remember other things about this day too.

It was a beautiful day with plenty of sunshine and nice breezes. It was the final day of the spring races at school so Rachel and I took David down in his stroller to cheer on my students, Weber's Warriors, as they ran. One of my girls earned a second-place finish in the sprint and my class team (two boys and two girls) won their relay race.

I know I'm going to remember feeling proud of my students as they gave it their all, and maybe a little extra because they knew the Littlest Warrior was watching them. I'm going to remember hoisting my winning team members onto my shoulder one at a time after the race so their classmates could cheer for them.

Lifting my students after the race has become a tradition of mine. I did this during my first year of teaching for a boy in my class who won the sprints. He loved being in the spotlight and, because he was a little smaller than some of his classmates, I was able to carry him around for a while, his face beaming the entire time. When I finally brought him back down, he looked up at me and told me how no man had ever lifted him up like that and said they were proud of him. I can look back on that moment and think it could have been the first time I was able to do something "dad-like" for a child.

At the time fatherhood wasn't even on my radar, but I had a brief glimpse of what it could be, the joy and pride that I could feel for a child that I had influenced in some way. I would have loved to carry David around like that one day.

Obituary:

David Christopher Weber, 11 months, the son of Phil and Rachel Weber, of Champaign, died at 10:40 p.m. on Thursday, May 29, 2008, at his home.

The family will receive visitors from 3 to 6 p.m. Sunday at the Heath Vaughn Funeral Home, in Champaign. The visitation will include a brief reading at 5:30 p.m.

In addition to his parents David is also survived by his

maternal grandparents, Rick and Jane Voyles, of Ashley, IL., his paternal grandparents, Peggy and Roscoe McPherren, of Bloomington, IL., his maternal aunt, Elizabeth Voyles, of Atlanta, GA., his paternal aunt and uncle, Ellen and Dan Groce, and their children Louie, Molly and Samantha Groce, all of Chenoa, IL. Other survivors include his Godparents, Darren and Jennifer Tee, and their children, Caroline, Drew and Gwen, all of Champaign, special friends Jill Kjorlien, Karen Ranney and Steve and Dena Hartke, all of Champaign, his friends at Miss Dena's and dozens of Weber's Warriors who have supported the family throughout this ordeal.

David was preceded in death by his paternal grandfather, Wayne H. Weber.

In lieu of flowers, memorials may be made to the Ronald McDonald House of St. Louis, MO. The family also has two other requests. First, they ask everyone to sign their organ donor card immediately and to make their wishes known to their families. Secondly, the Webers request that anyone who loved David honor his memory by going out of their way to bring a smile to someone else every day just as David brought so many smiles during his short life.

As always, thank you for your prayers, your good thoughts, and your positive energy.

After The End & What Comes Next?

June 2, 2008, 6:30 a.m.

Today is the day after David's funeral. I can't believe that I'm planning this, but I promised my students I'd try to be at the graduation ceremony they are having at school today. These kids have been with me through so much that I wouldn't feel right if I didn't attend. This is a big deal for them. They've worked hard to get here, and I'm proud of them. I'm going to be there for them just like they've been there for me.

It is going to be hard to say goodbye to these kids. I get very attached to my students anyway, but this year's bunch is different. There was a more intense bond with some of these kids because of how they reacted to all of the news about David.

June 14, 2008, 8:57 a.m.

I can't believe it's been more than two weeks. Two weeks without hearing his laugh or seeing him smile. Two weeks without feeling him fall asleep with his head against my shoulder. I never thought I'd say this, but I miss the way he smelled after a nap. Heck, I'd even settle for changing a diaper right about now, but that would be a second-tier wish at best.

Tomorrow would have been David's first birthday. This weekend is made even harder by the fact that Sunday is also Father's Day.

I'm not ready to stop being a dad.

Rachel and I have been staying busy for the past two weeks. Projects around the house let us keep our minds on doing something productive rather than wallowing in anger, grief, confusion, self pity, or other emotions that don't help anything. We're getting our house ready to sell so there are always plenty of things that need to be done. We're not leaving Champaign. There are just too many memories in our current house.

Every morning, I walk out of my bedroom and look down the hall expecting to see David sitting on his play mat in the living room. I expect him to be badly trying to stack plastic rings or pushing balls through his dragon playset and giggling when he can get the lights and sounds to come on. Even worse, I still expect him to look up and see me when I come around the corner and for him to give out a happy scream when he realizes I'm there.

Every morning, I have to remember that he's gone and he's not coming back.

I'll be heading back down to St. Louis next week. I'm going to meet with David's doctors and nurses one last time. I guess I need that kind of closure.

While I'm down there, I'm going to visit the Ronald McDonald House's Family Room in the hospital to drop off a big bag of pop-tops from soda cans that my students collected. The volunteers will probably make the same joke they always do, "I hope you didn't drink all this yourself." I'm sure I'll smile at the joke, just like I always do, then take one last look around. Having that room available helped me in so many ways. It was a great place for me to sit and write, but it was also a friendly place where I could be away from the hospital room for a little while, somewhere that I could be among a room full of other parents who were trying to give themselves a break, just like I was.

I'm also going to give the volunteers the checks for David's memorials. I'm pleased to say that people donated roughly $2,500 dollars in his name. I can think of no better way for David to be remembered than to think that donations in his name will help other families in similar situations to make the best of a bad time.

Everyone has been wonderful to us these past few months, but especially during these past two weeks. People have given us the space we need, but they've also been right there if we needed them. There have been dozens of little things that have made this experience a little easier: A kind word here or there, Rachel's company giving her a little extra time off, friends and family members sharing special photos, and dozens of other things that I can't list here.

One act of kindness that especially resonates with me and cheers me up whenever I think about it deserves special mention. On their last day of school, a time when they should be thinking about themselves and their plans for summer, the fifth-grade students at Kenwood went out of their way to do something nice for me, to remember David in the best possible way. They kicked off their final fifth-grade dance with The Chicken Dance as a way to commemorate David's obsession with the Japanese Silky Chicken at

Miller Park Zoo.

I knew my Warriors wouldn't let me down.

June 15, 2008 8:52 a.m.

Today would have been David's first birthday.

A friend sent me an e-mail yesterday with an interesting message. It told a story of three trees in the woods discussing what they would like to be when they "grew up."

The first tree said it wanted to be a treasure chest and hold the world's greatest treasure. The second tree said it wanted to be part of a great sailing ship that would be part of a vast fleet and carry kings. The third tree said it didn't want to be cut down at all. It wanted to keep growing until it reached the heavens and would be an inspiration to people everywhere.

A group of woodsmen and carpenters came into the woods one day and cut down all three trees. The first tree didn't become a treasure chest, it became a feeding trough for animals. Several years later the second tree become part of a ship, but it was a simple fishing boat instead of the flagship of a king's fleet. Finally, after roughly 30 years of sitting around unused, the wood from the third tree was used to create a cross upon which a man was hung.

It isn't hard to figure out the symbolism behind what these three trees became. I guess it is just a matter of changing one's perspective to see that all three trees fulfilled their destinies and their dreams in ways they couldn't imagine when they were still part of the forest.

That e-mail made sense to me and helped me realize that I needed to change my perspective on some things. After I thought about things for a while, I realized I'd been feeling like my tree had been cut down for no good reason at all. Maybe there really was a reason, I just haven't been able to see it yet because of my perspective. I just don't know.

That friend, a former student, taught me a lesson yesterday and I am grateful to her for reminding me to try to look at things in a different way.

I guess it is ironic, or perhaps destiny, that I am down in Southern Illinois today with Rachel's parents to plant a tree in David's name.

June 20, 2008 4:14 p.m.

I made what is probably my last trip down to St. Louis Children's Hospital on Thursday. I had to go to the Ronald McDonald House Family Room to drop off a wagonload (literally – a wagonload) of pop-tops and some checks we'd been given as memorials to David. I also met with David's doctors one last time to wrap up some unfinished business.

Sure, I could have mailed that stuff off but I felt that I had to do this in person. I guess I just needed to be there and, since I have nothing but time right now because of summer break, I decided that the time was right for a visit.

I'm proud of myself for being able to walk through those doors. I really wasn't sure I was going to be able to do it. I didn't give the matter much thought until I hit the bridge over the Mississippi River and started seeing landmarks that were so familiar from all of those trips down there with David.

My heart started beating a bit faster and my breath seemed to get stuck in my throat. For a brief while I thought I might have to call off my appointments with the doctors. Then the strangest thing happened. I pulled into the parking garage and a lot of that stress seemed to go away.

By the time I stepped off the elevator and heard the whistles from the model trains that circle the foyer, I had calmed down enough so that I only had a slight shaking in my hands. There is something about that place that is so comforting that I wasn't afraid to keep walking.

I saw plenty of familiar faces. There was the young guy behind the information desk who was always helpful, pointing me in the right direction for so many appointments, and there was the middle-aged woman who was a cashier in the cafeteria who seemed to make a point of smiling at each person who walked past her counter. I saw one of the nurses who we had bonded with and I recognized more than a few parents from their own long hospital stays.

Maybe it sounds cheesy but, when I finally got around to visiting the school room and the park-like area on the eighth floor, I realized that SLCH isn't only about healing children. Visiting David's hospital, seeing those places, and feeling the emotions they brought up within me, helped heal a wound that I didn't even know I had.

I think, maybe, I finally understand the concept of closure.

Even though I still hurt, and probably will for the rest of my life, the wound maybe isn't as open and raw now as it was before my trip. Could this be the first time that a trip to the hospital helped someone even before they ever saw a doctor?

June 28, 2008, 2:35 p.m.

I guess I should be used to having mixed feelings. It's been happening a lot these past few months.

We got a call today that we'd been waiting for (waiting and waiting and waiting actually). David's primary doctor from St. Louis called us today to say that the test results were in. David was mutation negative, which means that we do not need to worry about any other child we have coming down with this kind of cancer.

Whew! Of course, I was relieved. The possibility that any child we give birth to would have the same type of cancer was daunting. I don't think we could go through that again. Now we know that it won't happen.

Still, there is a downside to this new information. If David had been mutation positive then his death might have been easier to take, sort of. We could look at it as an inevitability if the doctor had said something like, "Well, given your unique genetic make-ups as parents, there was an 87 percent chance that he was going to have this problem." Maybe then we could have accepted it. You can't argue with those kinds of percentages.

Now, I'm left wondering how I should feel. We don't know what caused David to develop this kind of cancer. Given how rare this was (remember, fewer than 50 people in the world have had this kind of cancer start in their livers) I have to wonder why or how it formed. The odds were drastically against him getting any kind of cancer, but especially rhabdoid sarcomas. Why did he die? Was my son taken from me because of a fluke?

We were in the parking lot of Toys R Us when we got the call from the doctor. We were shopping for a "How to Play Guitar" book so I could work on another item on my Daddy-To-Do List Part II: Learn to play the guitar so you can play "Rainbow Connection" as a lullaby. I bought an acoustic guitar Friday, so now I need to figure out how to play. I'd always told myself that I wanted to learn how to play an instrument in time to impress David, perhaps even play lullabies for him. That would have been a cool Dad thing to do. I missed my chance, but I still want to learn.

After the call I was so confused and emotional that my hands were shaking and I half forgot why we were there. Rachel was ecstatic with the good news, but I was torn. Part of me wanted to do cartwheels but another part wanted to go someplace quiet so I could lie down.

I guess I'll never know why or how David developed his cancer. In the long run it probably doesn't really matter. It's kind of like knowing whether the bus that just hit you was painted red or blue. In the big picture, those details aren't as important. The end result is that you've still been hit by a bus.

It's just one more thing that's going to keep me up at night now and then.

June 28, 2008, 9:25 p.m.

Tonight I held a baby for the first time since David died in my arms. It hurt, but it wasn't impossible.

A good friend of ours invited us over for a cookout. Her 13-month-old son was, of course, in attendance. Now, don't get me wrong. I'd been around the baby several times since David's death. In fact, I spent a few hours with him this afternoon when his mother joined Rachel and I at the mall for a little shopping. I'd even tried to pick him up one other time, about a week or so ago, but he squirmed and yelled so I didn't push the issue.

When David died, we said we didn't want there to be any strangeness between us and this boy's family. Up until now, there hadn't been any. Tonight, however, my friend's son held his arms out to me and wanted me to pick him up.

It took me a few seconds to realize two things: First, I was being stupid. This was a great little boy who wanted me to play with him, something I'd been dreaming about for a while. Second: I wasn't breathing. Once I caught my breath I was able to pick him up and play. We laughed and it felt right. It reminded me of one of the reasons why I wasn't ready to give up being a dad. Laughing babies are a cure for almost anything.

July 4, 2008, 7:56 a.m.

The Fourth of July always used to be one of my favorite holidays, just behind Halloween, but I have a feeling that this year it is going to be a rough day. Every year I go back to the little town where I grew up. My whole family gets together at my sister's house and the entire town has a festive energy that happens all too rarely in small towns. Everybody is wearing red, white, and blue, and the town is decked out with streamers and flags and there is a big parade. The whole town seems to have a family/high school reunion feel to it because everybody who grew up there and moved away comes back for the afternoon. It's usually a pretty good time.

Last year was one of the best Independence Day's that I can remember. David was only about three weeks old. He was wearing a tiny little red, white and blue one-piece outfit that I referred to as his Captain America costume. I even made him a tiny little shield to go with it. Yeah, I'm that big of a nerd. The outfit was extra special because David's youngest God-sister picked it out so he could have something nice for the day.

I was every bit the picture of a proud daddy as I walked around town pushing a stroller that was so new that it didn't even squeak. I showed David off to my relatives that hadn't had a chance to see him yet. He was so little that my uncle was afraid to hold him. I even sought out old friends from high school just so I could brag about my son.

Today, that stroller, which has developed quite a few squeaks, is stuffed into a closet. The Captain America costume is packed away in a plastic tub that holds a few things of his we wanted to keep but not see every day.

What am I going to say when I see those same old high school friends today? How am I going to handle it when I have to tell them David is gone, and I have to see that look on their faces?

That look still gets me. That horrified look as the news sinks in and they realize what's happened makes it new for me too. I lose him all over again.

I know I don't have to go. It doesn't matter that about fifty people are going to be there waiting for me to bring potato salad. I can practically hear my sister saying, "The grocery store sells potato salad. It's no big deal. Come if you want, but you don't have to." I could skip it and nobody would blame me. My family and the friends who know what's going on would understand completely, and they wouldn't say or think anything against me for not showing up.

Staying home, though, wouldn't do any good. Instead of feeling bad at a family reunion, a flea market, or fireworks, I'd be feeling bad on my couch in Champaign. The only difference is that in Chenoa, I'd at least have a family reunion, a flea market, and fireworks to, maybe, take my mind off of things for a while and let me feel like a normal person again.

I can either sit around my house feeling sorry for myself or I can get off my butt and do something that might make the situation better. I'm going and I'm going to do my best to be in a good mood. At the very least, I'm going to do my best to fake it and see if those acting classes in college paid off.

July 22, 2008, 10:56 p.m.

I took the last of David's pictures down from the walls of my classroom this past week.

I've been trying to get ready for the new school year. I guess I thought it would be easier to keep myself together on rough days if I didn't have to see those pictures every day. I came in to the school quite a bit this past summer, largely because I wanted something to do, another project to keep myself occupied and to keep my mind off of David. Those first few visits were tough. My room had about a dozen pictures of him: Smiling David, Sleeping David, Playing David, and one of Eating David that a student had dubbed "That Snot Picture" because the green beans that were smeared across his face looked like the world's worst booger.

All of those pictures were looking at me when I walked into that room for the first time. It was like he had just died again.

Most of the pictures came down during my second summer visit. I'd only left a few of the more special photos up. Now, other than the one framed picture I have on my desk of David and Rachel together, he's not there anymore.

Well, I shouldn't say that. A pair of special initiatives by friends made certain that he will always be remembered at Kenwood Elementary. Both of those initiatives were discussed at a faculty meeting today.

The first program is something I've mentioned here before. Some of Rachel's friends and co-workers have endowed a scholarship/writing competition for fifth-grade students at Kenwood. For the next twelve years they are offering a $50 savings bond to the student who wins the David C. Weber Memorial Writing Competition.

As my part of the project, I showed off a plaque I had made. The winners will have their names engraved on a nice wooden plaque that will hang in the school's main hallway. I was very impressed with the trophy shop's work. The plaque has an etched picture of David next to his name.

The second initiative that was announced today was one that I wasn't aware of. Two of my students from last year approached the principal just before school let out for the summer (David's funeral was the day before vacation started). These two young men asked if they could start a fund to have a tree planted on the playground in David's name. They both gave five $1 bills as a way to start things off.

When the principal made this announcement today I was stunned. These boys could have used that money to have some fun over the summer: admission to the pool or a hot dog during a ball game. Instead they were thinking of David and wanted to do something nice, just like their classmates who wrote me letters, saved pop-tops, donated to David's memorial fund at SLCH and a dozen other acts of kindness.

I've said it before, but this is just another example of how my Warriors won't let me down.

July 25, 2008, 2:30 p.m.

I had to tell someone about David today. They hadn't heard yet.

I ran into the mother of a former student at school. She was picking up one of her younger children from his first day at kindergarten. Her daughter had been in my class while Rachel was pregnant. In fact, her daughter gave David one of his first outfits, a little shirt for a newborn that said "Handsome" on it. This girl was from the class that all referred to David as "D.C." because I told them the story about how I was such a nerd that I wanted my son's initials to be those of the comic book company.

Anyway, this mom knew from school bulletins and parent scuttlebutt last year (the year after her daughter was in my class) that David had been sick. I don't know if she knew exactly how sick though because, after a few seconds of "How are you?" and "Are you ready for the school year?" small-talk, she asked me how David was doing.

She had a small, hopeful smile when she asked and her head was cocked in a way that I've come to associate with someone who is expecting to hear good news and a cute baby story. Obviously, she had to be thinking that if I was able to make cheery-sounding small-talk everything must be okay. I guess she could tell by the way I took a sharp breath before I spoke that things weren't as good as she'd hoped and that the news wasn't something she'd want to hear.

I tried to sound strong even though I was suddenly feeling pretty weak. I said, "Um … He, ah … He didn't make it." I think my voice cracked somewhere in that sentence. For a split-second it was like I'd just lost him again and I was calling family or close friends to tell them. My hands started to shake and my eyes started to burn. I could feel a lump forming in my throat.

She was clearly shocked and might have mumbled something about being sorry. I can't quite remember exactly what was said during those few awkward seconds. I coughed to give myself a bit of extra time to recover my composure. I remember making an apology to her.

That's strange, isn't it? She unknowingly brought up a very painful subject and I apologized to her because my reaction made her feel awkward.

Is there a good way to handle conversations about death? Does anyone feel comfortable with this subject, especially when it is fresh? Maybe funeral home directors can handle it and maybe adults that are dying can handle it, but I don't know if anyone else can.

July 26, 2008, 11:00 a.m.

I keep thinking ahead to the next event that will signify when I should be "over this" and "done with the grieving process." It seems like I keep looking to an event like David's first birthday, Independence Day, the start of school, etc., and I keep thinking that these events are going to mark some kind of turning point for me. Somehow after "This Event" then I'll be okay. It doesn't matter what the event is. The only thing that matters is that, in future years, I'll be able to look back and say that "This Event" marked the beginning of the end of my grieving stage.

I'm in Chicago this weekend. Rachel's company is hosting a business meeting here and I took a train up to spend the weekend with Rachel. It's another event, another chance for me to move on.

Is this part of the bargaining stage? Have I twisted that stage around so that I am bargaining with grief rather than bargaining with death? Somehow, I don't think this weekend trip to Chicago is going to be the turning point that I'm waiting for.

I guess I should be used to seeing fathers and sons out together. It still seems to get me though. The strange thing is that today it was a boy and his dad that I couldn't even see that got to me. I could only hear them. That was enough.

I was in a bookstore downtown looking over the bargain bins hoping to find a cheap book about pro-wrestling that is appropriate for ten-year-olds. One of my students had asked me to add some books on "rasslin'" to my class library, so I was determined to find a deal.

I wasn't looking too closely at the titles, just killing time really while Rachel looked at the art books on a different floor.

I heard a tiny voice from a few aisles over say, "Daddy, look at this. I want to show you something." I could hear the smile in his father's answering voice when he said, "This must be a good day. This is the third thing you've had to show me so far."

The little boy gave a precocious giggle, as if this was a common joking complaint of his father's. I heard the boy's feet running on the carpeted floor in the other direction, a staggering run of a boy who isn't all that graceful and who may be wearing shoes that are a bit too big. I'd imagine that the boy was, at best, four years old, an estimate based solely on the sound of his voice and his footsteps. I have to estimate because I couldn't make myself look.

Part of me really wanted to peek around the corner, wanted to see this happy scene being played out in the basement of a bookstore. Still, I couldn't do it.

Somehow, I knew that, no matter what the boy actually looked like, I'd see David. I'd see what my son should have looked like three years from now. The boy would have had light brown hair, slightly curly and maybe a bit too long. He'd have had puffy cheeks, brown eyes and dimples, maybe just one dimple showing unless he was really smiling, like his mom.

No matter what that boy in the bookstore actually looked like to everybody else, I know what I would have seen. I know how he would have looked to me and I don't know if I could have taken it. I'm not sure if I could have looked at that little boy being playfully chased by his father and still kept myself under control.

I didn't look. I didn't peek around the corner because I was afraid of my reaction. I was afraid of how I would look if I started to get choked up in public. So much for, "Live Without Fear From Now On." Maybe that's like Kramer's vow of silence on "Seinfeld" … it starts, NOW!

Aug. 7, 2008, 4:15 p.m.

A strange thing keeps happening this week. It seems like every time I turn around something significant happens to remind me of David.

I just found a picture of him in an unlabeled file on my computer at work. To have him unexpectedly looking back at me from the screen was a bit of a shock. Last night, I ran into a former student who wanted to talk about David but, at the same time, really did not want to talk about him because she kept getting upset. She couldn't even say his name without choking up.

This morning a child from first or second grade came up to me and asked if I was the man whose baby had died. Honestly, what I am I supposed to say to that? I did my best. I said, "Yes, I am. Thank you for caring," and then I moved on.

Out of the blue today one of my new students made a point of telling me that his birthday is June 15, the same day as David's. We hadn't been talking about birthdays or David. We were in the middle of a math lesson. I have no idea why that new topic of conversation came up. He raised his hand, waited patiently for me to call on him and then said something like, "That reminds me … my birthday is June 15." Holy crap! Where did that come from?

The final and strangest thing came when I was fishing in my pocket for some change to buy a soda during lunch. I do this almost every day without any odd consequences or occurrences. Today, however, was different. One of the coins I had in my pocket was actually a token from the carousel at the Miller Park Zoo. I saved that token as a memento of our first trip there. I keep it in my wallet so I can have something special of his with me at all times. It must have fallen out, but why now? Why did it happen on this day?

I'm finding lately that simple things are becoming more complicated and it becomes much harder to concentrate because so many things remind me of my son. I'm constantly being pulled out of the moment and taken back to the day he died. It's been several weeks now. Will this kind of thing happen forever or will it, someday, get better?

Aug. 19, 2008, 6:30 p.m.

I'm still amazed at how a little thing can throw off my entire day. I can hear a song on the radio, see a baby and his daddy walking together, or even simply speak to the wrong person at the wrong time and I can be in a funk all day.

Today, a young student came up to me during breakfast at school. He smiled strangely and gave me a hug around the waist. Although I've never had this child in class, I know who he is. He's a sweet boy and this kind of thing happens frequently, especially with younger students. It doesn't take much for a child to want to give a teacher a hug. It can mean that they are happy to see you or it could just mean that they are in a good mood and are happy to be in school.

When the hug was over, the boy pulled back and looked up at me with a sad expression on his face. With a slightly quivering lower lip, he said, "I'm sorry your baby died."

My day might as well have ended right there and it wasn't even 7:30 a.m. yet. Children can still get me like this. Adults usually have a "tell" that lets me know they are about to say something about David. They pause, sigh, and look away for a second before they speak. It is usually enough for me to prepare myself so I'm not hit as hard by whatever it is they are about to say. Children, however, are not as complicated as adults. They don't have the forethought to know that what they are about to say may bring some pain to the person they are talking to. All they know is that they are sad and they want to tell someone that they care.

God bless them for that.

Thankfully today was a half day.

The situation at school was even stranger because I was teaching the book *Hatchet* again and was almost to the Mr. Perpich part. Today was the first time I've had to teach that particular lesson since my own Mr. Perpich moments with David. I had to tell my students about the power of a positive attitude on a day when my own attitude had already taken a few hits.

It is time for me to restock my own lacking enthusiasm. I have to repair the gaping holes in my emotional armor, but I have to do it in such a way that I don't go too far. I don't want to shield myself so much that I become cut off. Like Mr. Perpich would say, I have to get up off my butt and do something to make my situation better.

I'm starting a special healing step tonight. I'm crossing off another item on my "Daddy To Do" list. Tonight I'm taking my first guitar lesson. I'm going to learn how to play "The Rainbow Connection." This is the song that always takes me back to the best and the worst times of my life because I used to sing it for David while I got him ready for bed.

Shortly after Rachel told me she was pregnant I made a promise. I was going to learn how to play an instrument, preferably a guitar, because I wanted my son to grow up in a house with live music. I also wanted to be the "Cool Dad who plays guitar" and rocks out at birthday parties. I always thought I'd have plenty of time to learn. He was only a baby, right? He won't appreciate music or rockin' Dad until he's a little older, right?

I know my step is coming too late for David to hear me play, but I hope it isn't too late for me to earn a bit of forgiveness (even if it is only forgiving myself) for failing to keep this promise to my son.

Aug. 20, 2008, 8:30 p.m.

I took another step today, maybe even a step and a half. I watched David's video for the first time.

A few months ago, when the end was coming near, my good friends Jill Kjorlien and Lee Alexander took the home movies and still photos of David and edited them together with some of our favorite songs to make a special video that we could play during his funeral. I haven't been able to bring myself to watch it. That changed today.

I finally felt like I was ready. It was rough, but it was good. The home movies were set apart by time stamps so the viewer could tell exactly when each video was shot. At first it was great, but I quickly started looking at those time stamps as a countdown. I knew the end was coming and it became harder and harder to watch as his hair fell out and he started losing weight.

It made me smile and cry at the same time to hear him laugh again. I noticed that his smile and his laugh didn't change. He loved life as long as he had it. Seeing him again was both hurtful and helpful, kind of like reopening an old wound in order to clean it so the real healing can begin.

It needed to happen. The time finally seemed right.

Nov. 23, 2008, 9:14 p.m.

It has been quite a while since I've updated this journal.

I could have written about the memorial service that St. Louis Children's Hospital presented to the parents and what it was like to sit in that church with the families of cancer patients who didn't survive. I could have written about the times when students have asked to see pictures of David. I really almost did write about the time earlier this week when I looked in the pocket of a heavy coat and found one of the surgical-style masks I had to wear last winter so I wouldn't infect David with the flu.

That last one hit me out of the blue. It left me standing in the parking lot at school gasping for breath, suddenly unsure of where I was and what I had been doing.

On the other, more positive hand, I could have also written about the wonderful support people continue to give us. I could have mentioned how I've started passing out tokens for the carousel to strangers at the mall, my way of helping someone else maybe make a memory or two, maybe cross something off of their Daddy To Do list …

Ultimately, I didn't write journal entries about any of those things. I guess I was waiting for the perfect thing to say. Now that the day-to-day ups and downs are mostly done, I wondered if I had anything important left to write about.

Well, I think I finally found the right thing to write. I'm going to be a daddy again because Rachel is pregnant.

It was a rocky beginning. We thought she was pregnant for a while but all of the at-home tests she took were inconclusive. "Is that a second line or not? It looks kinda like a line, but it isn't as solid as that other line. What does all this mean?"

Rachel scheduled a blood test and it showed that she was pregnant but it was very early on. A second blood test about a week later showed that Rachel had suffered a miscarriage. The pregnancy hormone in her blood had dropped to almost nothing. About two weeks later, the doctors performed a third blood test to be certain we were safe to continue trying to become pregnant. Uh-oh … um, that test showed that she was 100 percent, without a doubt, five weeks pregnant.

We were worried. What could cause the hormone levels to drop that sharply and then rocket back up? It was possible that she was having an ectopic or molar pregnancy? We scheduled an ultrasound and some other tests and everything is OK. The baby is where it should be and things are progressing normally.

I guess you have to be at least 5 feet, 8 inches to ride this emotional roller coaster. I just made it.

March 11, 2009, 6:12am

I guess I'm going to have to get used to seeing the color pink around the house more often. No, I'm not revisiting my *Risky Business* fashion sense from the mid-80's. We are having a girl.

We're very excited. We found out at about 4 o'clock Friday afternoon and by noon Saturday, this baby already had about $150 worth of cute frilly clothes, and that's just the clothes we know about. She has aunts, grandparents and several "adopted" aunts & uncles that have already said they were waiting with credit cards ready for the pink/blue update.

We've decided to name her Margaret Jane after her grandmothers, but we'll probably call her Maggie. The name has already brought a lump to my throat and she hasn't even had it for a whole week yet. Last night a friend took me to see "Movin' Out," the musical based on Billy Joel's songs, and during one part of the show a woman is on stage alone doing a bit of ballet. I was reminded of the song "At The Ballet" from *A Chorus Line* (a show I did in college). The song includes the lyrics "... And he'd say 'Maggie, do you want to dance?' and I'd say, 'Daddy, I would love to.'"

Anyway, I always thought that was a really sweet moment in the show and soon I will have my own Maggie to ask to dance. Something new for my "Daddy-To-Do" list.

May 10, 2009, 12:09 a.m.

Today was a good day. That's an odd thing because a year ago today, I didn't know if I'd ever say that again. It was almost exactly a year ago that we were told David had only three weeks to live.

We commemorated this event/anniversary/whatever by

planting a redbud tree in a nearby park. There is a little bronze plaque right next to the tree (a plaque that at this moment is decorated with dandilions, the only flowers David's god-siblings could easily find to pick at the park without getting in trouble).

The park is across the street and down the block. It's where we used to take David to watch baseball games with my students (my other kids). Sure, he didn't get into the games all that much but he liked being outside in the nice weather and it always made for a nice evening or afternoon in the park.

It was at this park where I stopped by to see some of my students on the day David was born. I was on my way home to pick up a few things to take back to Rachel at the hospital and, being a little caught up on the moment, I completely missed my turn and ended up right next to the park. I couldn't resist sharing the good news.

I got there just in time because the game had either just ended or it was just about to begin. Either way, the timing was great because I was able to talk to the boys. I ran up and said, "Hey guys, I'm a dad!" I got a round of high-fives and a few hugs and then quickly headed back to the hospital.

I'm going to think of that moment, one of the proudest moments of my life, every time I see that tree.

I'm sitting here at my computer, typing with a cheesy grin on my face, remembering all those good times at that park. It's strange because I really thought I'd be upset today. Luckily I had Rachel and some good friends around during the planting and during the afternoon to keep my spirits up.

Today was a good day.

May 25, 2009, 7:47 p.m.

We had another tree planting for David on Saturday. It was very nice. The Kenwood School PTA sponsored some fundraising to pay for the project, which was originally suggested by two of my students from last year.

We planted an October glory maple on the school playground. In about a week we're going to put in a plaque. Overall it was a very nice experience. Several friends and family members showed up to help us plant. Several of my students were on hand to help water the tree once it was in the ground.

I was asked to say a few words once the tree was set up. What follows is a rough transcript of my speech:

"Today is about people who really do care, the friends and family who really do make a difference. I think it is fitting that this tree is being planted here, where the Kenwood Cross Country race begins. It was at this race in 2007 that David was first introduced to many of his Kenwood family. Rachel was still on maternity leave and she wheeled him down to school in the stroller so my students could meet him.

"The students in my class and throughout the school all seemed to like hearing stories about David. They liked seeing the new pictures I'd put up on my classroom – even the

137

disgusting pictures of his first try eating peas seemed to bring a few smiles. When David got sick, the people in this school rallied around us in a way that we will never be able to repay. The Kenwood family and Weber's Warriors didn't let us down.

"David came back to Kenwood for the relay races at the end of the year. He'd been pretty much out of it for a while because he was on so much pain medication, but that day he knew exactly where he was. He enjoyed seeing the kids and being where the action was.

"As we were preparing for the end, our hospice nurse told us that often it seems like people wait for a certain event before they can let go, before they believe it is OK for them to die. They have one last something that has to be done. I believe that, for David, that one last something was seeing the students at this school one last time. He was happy here that day.

"He died later that night.

"The plaque that will accompany this tree has the phrase, 'Always Ride the Carousel.' To me, that means that we shouldn't wait to do those important things in life that make life worth living. We never know when things can end, so why waste time? Why waste time and energy being concerned with those false and insincere people when there are so many more important things, more important people, in life?

"Riding the carousel at the mall was one of the things on my Daddy-To-Do List that I got to do because I didn't wait. David's first trip on the carousel was probably one of the best days of his life. It was also the day they told us he had less than a year to live, so it was one of the worst days of my life. I guess it's just a matter of perspective. I'll treasure that time and that memory for as long as I live.

"When you leave here today I want you to think of the special people in your life and the things you've put off saying or doing because there's always time for that later, right? Think of those people and then ride the carousel."

March 28, 2010, 11:55 p.m.

Maggie is doing well. She's a little more than eight months old and growing into a healthy and happy baby girl. There doesn't seem to be any hints of anything wrong with her. Her doctors, who know her family history, have been very good about looking for problems that would be unexpected for anyone else.

Maggie is about to do a bunch of things ... she's about to start crawling. She's about to get her first tooth. She's about to start waving hello. She's about to start growing hair (I hope). She's about to drive her father nuts with all the things she's about to do but isn't quite doing yet.

The only thing she's doing on a regular basis is giving kisses. Man, I love those.

I've just ended a week of daddy-daughter time where I was off of school for Spring Break and daycare wasn't operating. I'm exhausted at the end of every day but it is a really good kind of exhausted. We've spent our days playing peek-a-boo, rolling balls, taking walks in the stroller, trying to practice crawling, tickling, and fighting against taking naps.

It's been great. I guess it makes me wonder about the big "Might-Have-Been." Maggie is so much like David that it hurts sometimes. Still, she is her own person.

Maggie gets the same kind of crinkled up nose look on her face that David used to get. With David, it seemed to mean that he was up to something and that he was about to be ornery. I get the same look on my face when I'm about to be ornery so I know exactly what that look meant. With Maggie, that same look seems to mean something different. She crinkles up her nose and looks at me as if to say, "Man, you really are an idiot!"

Come to think of it, her mom gets that same look fairly frequently.

I want to ask everyone for a favor: Sign your organ donor cards when you renew your drivers' licenses. Cancer is a tricky thing and there are never any guarantees when you are dealing with cancer, but David's doctors tell us that it is possible that David could still be alive today if they could have found an eligible donor two years ago.

I know it isn't fair to ply you with stories about how cute Maggie is and compare her to how cute David was and then ask you to do something icky like think about your own mortality and how harvesting organs can be gross. Cancer isn't fair and I'm going to fight just as dirty as cancer does. Sign the card.

Do the right thing. Do it now while you are thinking about it. Maybe if you do that then David's death will mean something. Maybe he died so that you could sign your card and that will, in turn, save someone who will cure cancer someday. For the record, I signed my card before David was ever born and, when the time came, I signed David's card for him. His organs were taken so they could be studied in the hopes of finding a cure.

I'm not asking you to do anything we haven't already done.

Jan. 15, 2011, 12:00 a.m.

It's been close to a year since I last updated this journal. Things are going well. The act of getting by day-to-day has shifted into something closer to breakdowns that happen week-to-week. I guess that's progress.

Maggie is doing very well. At a year and a half old she is healthy and happy and she is doing everything that parents want children to do as long as they are somebody else's children. She runs, she jumps, she cries, and she climbs stairs with reckless abandon. She screams that piercing baby-girl scream, she laughs unreservedly, and she eats enthusiastically, never-mind those odd times when she almost, sorta, kinda chokes a little bit when she stuffs her mouth a little too full. She does everything that young children do to drive their parents nuts ... and she loves it. I have to admit that I kinda like it too - other than the choking part because that still scares the crap out of me.

I tell myself that it is OK to be a bit nervous. Having lost one child already, I have to fight against my instinct to be over-protective. I try to turn that instinct into something pseudo-positive. I tell myself that I've already seen the worst that can happen so I'm not going to be freaked out by a fever, a stumble down a single stair, or a rough-sounding cough ... yeah right. That sounds like garbage even as I type it, but I guess if I say it to myself often enough I might, someday, come to believe it.

I'm just as nervous as any other relatively new dad. Once Maggie hit a year old she was in uncharted territory for me so all bets are off.

Maggie is just getting old enough that she is recognizing babies everywhere and she loves them. She gladly and loudly points them out at the mall, on TV, in her toy chest, on magazine covers, everywhere. She pointed one out at daycare the other day. It was a picture of David.

That was rough.

That was one of those times when getting by day-to-day or even week-to-week quickly turned into minute-by-minute, and I was left hoping that nobody saw me, or at least nobody with more than a five-word vocabulary. Maggie reached out and hugged me fiercely at that moment. I'm probably reading too much into it, but it seemed like she knew I needed something right about then.

We don't have a lot of pictures of David up at home. I'm not sure why. I have them up at school and Rachel has them at work. I guess having pictures up at home would hit too close to home, so to speak. I can keep myself together when I'm at work because I can't let myself lose control in front of students. I don't have those restrictions at home. It still doesn't take much for me to lose myself during unguarded moments. Maybe it will always be that way.

Overall, I guess life is moving on. I still take special notice of the tree we planted for David on the school grounds. Now that the leaves area all gone, I can clearly see the toy of his I hung on the branches last May as I drive up every morning. I guess it is progress that I can continue driving without having a big problem. Maybe someday I'll progress to the point where I can actually breathe as I drive by.

May 29, 2011, 10:17 p.m.

In about twenty minutes it will be exactly three years that he's been gone. I know it is sick, but that's what I've been doing today ... counting down the minutes. I've tried to keep myself busy, shopping, gardening, cooking, etc., but really that's all I've been doing today ... counting down until 10:40 p.m.

I guess this is a little morbid. I'm not sure why I do it. Today is worse than most. I have a hard time getting past that moment when David died. He was sitting on my lap. Even though Rachel and I were there and talking to him, telling him that we loved him, he was confused. He struggled to continue breathing and he was scared, terrified of leaving.

The look on his face at that exact moment is what wakes me up at night. He was scared and there was nothing I could do about it.

143

Nothing I'll ever do, regardless of the level of success or failure I reach in any part of my life, nothing will ever make up for that moment when there was nothing I could do to make his last moment better. That's something I'm going to have to live with.

Today I did what my psychologist suggested (yes, I'm seeing a shrink now and, yeah, it's about time). I wrote a note to David and released it with a helium balloon this afternoon. I guess it is supposed to be a symbolic gesture to say goodbye, to help me get past living in the past. I also left flowers at his memorial tree, the closest thing we have to a real gravesite. I said a little prayer (I don't do that very often) and made my little offering. I don't know if that was symbolic or not, but it made me feel a little better, so I guess it was worth doing.

The other thing I did today was that I spent the day trying to make Maggie laugh, which isn't an easy task with a teething two-year-old. I can't think of a better way to honor the child I lost then by enjoying the child I have. I try to be the dad to Maggie that I wanted to be for David. The only thing I can do for him now is show him (if he's watching) what I'd wanted for him.

Maggie didn't understand why I would let my balloon go when they are so much more fun to hold on to. She didn't understand why I didn't want to run around the school yard like she did. It was a beautiful afternoon, who wouldn't want to run? Still, on some level, I think maybe Maggie did understand that I was having a tough time. She was more generous with her hugs than she's been lately, more willing to laugh during goofy games we play.

Maybe she didn't understand what was going on with me today. Maybe she just understood that I needed a hug. That was enough. Some days that's all I've got.

In the next few weeks, I'm going to try a few more things my doctor suggested. Most importantly Rachel and I are going to celebrate David's birthday (June 15). We've never done that before. David died two weeks before his first birthday, so he never had a real birthday party. The doctor thinks that would be a big step, giving me something beyond May 29 to look forward to. I'll celebrate his birth rather than mourn his death. That sounds like a positive step and it feels right.

Oh yeah, the irony isn't lost on me. As I was typing this journal entry the exact 10:40 p.m. moment has come and gone. I guess writing this journal was just one of the many steps I took today to avoid thinking about what was really important.

Part II

Everything Else

Author's Note:

If you've been reading this book from the beginning you know what I've done, how I felt, and overall how I've dealt with David's situation. Right or wrong, that's how I did it. I know I made some mistakes that I hope you don't repeat but, if you do make the same mistakes I did (the Southern Comfort night sticks in my head for some reason) then know that you are not alone.

From here on, however, I've interviewed some top national experts in their fields to see how things usually go with families experiencing similar situations. For this portion of the book, I put on one of my old hats, the journalist cap to be precise, and asked a wide range of questions. Hopefully, their answers will help in ways that the previous section of the book couldn't by providing information from genuine experts.

Many of the people interviewed here had some part to play in David's case, while others are working in other hospitals with other children, but they are all important parts of the overall picture. I tried to get them to talk in generalities so their comments could relate to a wide range of problems for a wide range of families.

I hope this helps.

Who's Who:

Dr. Justin N. Baker: Dr. Baker holds three positions at St. Jude Children's Research Hospital in Memphis, Tennessee: director of the division of Palliative and End-of-Life Care, attending physician in the Quality of Life Service, and director of the Hematology/Oncology Fellowship Program. He is one of only a handful of physicians across the country with board certification in pediatrics, pediatric hematology/oncology, and hospice and palliative medicine.

Dr. ZoAnn Dreyer: Dr. Dreyer is a pediatric oncologist and the director of the Longterm Survivor Program at Texas Children's Hospital in Houston, Texas.

Dr. Ross W. Shepherd: Dr. Shepherd was the head of David's transplant team. He is the medical director of the liver program at St. Louis Children's Hospital and a professor with the departments of pediatrics, gastroenterology, and nutrition at Washington University.

Dr. Sharon McDonald: Dr. McDonald was David's primary doctor at St. Louis Children's Hospital. She is a fellow physician with the department of hematology/oncology at Washington University.

Dr. Kurt Soell: Dr. Soell is a psychologist/psychotherapist in the St. Louis, Missouri Area. He provides group, family, and individual therapy for children and young adults with cancer. He works closely with Friends of Kids with Cancer.

Rev. Brent Powell: Rev. Powell is the director of chaplain services for St. Jude Children's Research Hospital in Memphis, Tennessee. He oversees a team of chaplains who help guide patients, families, and hospital staff in moral, spiritual, religious, and ethical discussions.

Helene Morgan: Ms. Morgan is a clinical social worker on the Comfort and Palliative Care team at Los Angeles Children's Hospital. The team, which consists of physicians, oncologists, psychiatrists, nurses, and others to support the families as they have medical discussions, make symptom management, and end-of-life decisions, and conduct bereavement support.

Judy Ciapciak: Ms. Ciapciak is the executive director of Friends of Kids with Cancer, an organization that has provided education services, specialized recreational opportunities, and emotional therapy for children, teens, and their families in the St. Louis area for more than 20 years.

Lennell Jackson is a licensed social worker at St. Louis Children's Hospital. She works primarily with liver transplant patients.

Kelly Olson is also a licensed social worker at St. Louis Children's Hospital. She works primarily with cancer patients and their families on the hematology/oncology unit. Olson met with us frequently during our time at SLCH.

Lisa Gildehaus: Ms. Gildehaus is the kidney and liver transplant coordinator for St. Louis Children's Hospital. She oversees the entire transplant process, including scheduling procedures and generally serving as a liaison between families and the hospital.

Susan Basile: Ms. Basile is a senior transplant financial coordinator for St. Louis Children's Hospital. She works with parents to cover financial concerns relating to surgeries and hospital stays.

Judith Hicks: Ms. Hicks is a licensed social worker at St. Jude Children's Research Hospital. She helps families manage the demands of treatment and learn new ways to manage stress.

Amy Kennedy: Ms. Kennedy is a child life specialist at St. Jude Children's Research Hospital. Child Life specialists work to minimize the stress and anxiety that many kids have when they have to stay in the hospital.

Alicia Huettel: Ms. Huettel is the coordinator of the Family Centered Care Nursing Administration and a registered nurse at St. Jude Children's Research Hospital. She also helps oversee the hospital's Family Advisory Council, a committee of family members of patients, faculty and staff that seeks answers to the direct needs of patients and their parents by seeking their input and responding in kind.

Betsy Lambert is a member of the St. Jude Children's Research Hospital Family Advisory Council. She serves as a mentor to parents who are new to the hospital system as part of the Parents Assisting Inspiring and Reassuring (P.A.I.R.) team.

Malise Culpepper is a member of the St. Jude Children's Research Hospital Family Advisory Council. She serves as a mentor to parents who are new to the hospital system as part of the Parents Assisting Inspiring and Reassuring (P.A.I.R.) team.

Mrs. Lambert and Mrs. Culpepper are both are active in the Family Advisory Council.

Kathryn Berry-Carter: Ms. Berry-Carter is the director of Volunteer Services at St. Jude Children's Research Hospital. In this capacity, Kathryn is responsible for training volunteers about the needs and sensitivities of our patients and their families. She also directs the Parenting Mentoring Program, an effort to match families new to St. Jude's with others to help build a support network.

The First Few Days: Learning to Accept the Unacceptable

"Diseases desperate grown, by desperate appliances are relieved, or not at all,"

Claudius, from William Shakespeare's *Hamlet*

Okay, so your child has been diagnosed with something serious. It could be cancer or it could be one of a million other things that can go wrong. Regardless of the cause, unless it is the kind of thing that requires prompt action, such as an auto accident or impending immediate organ failure, you probably have at least a few days to sit and think.

How can I describe the worst feeling in the world? How can I tell someone what it is like to learn that your child has a serious, possibly life-threatening, illness? Well, if you are reading this book you probably already know what that feels like. Let's face it. This isn't beach-reading material. You didn't buy this book because you thought it looked like a real page-turner. You picked it up because you, or someone you know, are going through a similar situation and, by now, you've probably already had someone tell you that your child is sick.

Trust me. This is going to be a rough couple of days.

Every parent's situation is unique, just as their children and their medical situations are unique, but there are a few benchmarks most of us hit during these first few days after an initial diagnosis.

We all feel confused. We all feel scared and most of us, especially a lot of dads for some reason, feel a little bit angry. These feelings are normal.

Some cancers, like leukemia and lymphoma, are unfortunately common enough that they don't take too long to diagnose. Cancers like these can have a quick turn around when designing treatments. The protocols are in place. It stinks. There shouldn't be a series of thought-out, studied, and relied-upon treatments like these for children, but there are. I'm sorry. It's not your fault.

Solid tumor cancers, like David's, can take a lot longer to identify, thus the wait between diagnosis and treatment can be longer. Each comes with its own set of challenges and complications, but there are enough similarities between them that I'm not going to spend a lot of time nit-picking between the various types.

We're in the same club. God help us.

Something I found that helped me was to look for other parents who have had similar experiences, people who have some idea what it is like to go through what I was going through. It may feel like you're alone, but there are more of us out there than there should be. I tell people that, because of the uniqueness of their situation, I've never been exactly where they are, but I've been in the neighborhood enough that I know my way around. I guess it helps to know that you really aren't alone.

Betsy Lambert and Malise Culpepper are two of the volunteers on the St. Jude P.A.I.R. (Parents Assisting, Inspiring, and

Reassuring) committee. Both women have children receiving cancer treatment at St. Jude. Their job with the committee is to serve as mentors for parents who are just starting out on their journeys. Like all parents facing childhood cancer, they both said confusion and (hopefully brief) feelings of hopelessness are part of the process. I agree, especially about the hopelessness – but just because it starts out that way doesn't mean it has to stay that way forever. Lambert said that she was so lost that she forgot her own Social Security number while checking into the hospital for the first time. They both said finding someone who had been through a similar experience was a lifesaver. If nothing else, they found value in learning that they were not alone, and that their feelings were normal.

"When I heard that word (cancer) I think I froze. Everything stopped." Lambert said. "I was a wreck. I totally shut down. I didn't want to talk to anyone. I felt so alone. I told (my husband) that I want someone to talk to who has been through this."

Culpepper agreed. "This is going to be the hardest thing you've ever done, but you are going to be okay," she said.

Katherine Berry-Carter is the director of volunteer services at St. Jude. As such, she oversees the P.A.I.R. program and the Family Advisory Council (a volunteer group of parents who help make facility-wide recommendations at St. Jude.) Most hospitals, especially those large enough to have a pediatric oncology unit, will likely have someone like Carter on staff. She said these mentors – people like Culpepper and Lambert, are goldmines of information and can help newly diagnosed parents navigate the hospital system.

Finding a mentor, even an informal mentor that isn't part of an established program, can be important.

"There is nobody like another parent who has walked in those shoes, who has taken that journey," she said. "Hospital staff can't do that. Doctors can't do that, and volunteers can't do that. Only another parent can really know what you are going through."

The majority of parents approached about P.A.I.R. at St. Jude accept a mentor. Still, Lambert understands that if an initial offer is rejected, the door will usually remain open. "The ones who say 'no' are the ones who are so shocked that they may not know what they need yet," she said.

Hospitals without these mentor services on-site will likely have contacts with local organizations that can provide similar services even though they are not formally part of the hospital. While we were at St. Louis Children's Hospital we were hooked up with the St. Louis-based organization Friends of Kids with Cancer.

Judy Ciapciak, the executive director of Friends of Kids with Cancer, said her organization, and probably others like it in other metropolitan areas, can provide that extra bit of support for parents and families.

"We bring the parents (of cancer patients) together. You have friends to support you, but they don't really understand. We bring the parents together so they can laugh and cry together. They really get it," Ciapciak said.

Support groups, including those for siblings, exist everywhere. I recommend avoiding internet-based groups unless they are associated with a major hospital or professional organization. Even face-to-face groups aren't always perfect. If you are going that route make sure the group is a good fit for you or for your family. These groups are supposed to help you feel better. It isn't worth the effort if going becomes a source of stress.

Dr. ZoAnn Dreyer is a pediatric oncologist and the director of the Longterm Survivor Program at Texas Children's Hospital. She suggests turning to groups like the National Cancer Institute or the Children's Oncology Group for any research or recommendations.

Dr. Sharon McDonald, David's primary doctor at St. Louis Children's Hospital, said dads sometimes have a harder time with a serious, possibly life-threatening, diagnosis than moms do. In general, men want to fix things and women want to share things. That's a problem that relationship experts have cited for years. Dads typically want to be able to solve a problem right away.

"Most fathers are in the 'what can I do to fix this?' role. It's hard for them to relinquish that. The child goes to Dad when the bike is broken and to Mom when they cut their knee," Dr. McDonald says. "Fathers want to have some control over the uncontrollable."

I would tend to categorize dads into two areas during these first few days: Action Dad and Thinker Dad.

The Action Dad is the guy who wants to get right into treatment. He cannot stand the idea of sitting around. Action Dad wants to start taking steps immediately, even if they are small steps. "Do something" seems to be the motto of the Action Dad. I picture Action Dad as the guy in those old movies – his wife is about to give birth so they send him out to boil water. The doctors and nurses didn't need the water, they needed to give him something to do so he'd get out of their way yet still feel like he was helping. The fact that I kept a journal throughout the process and that I wrote this book is proof enough for me that I am probably an Action Dad. Even though I'm an Action Dad, I don't think one kind is better than the other. It is all about your personality and how you deal with these situations.

One of my favorite parts of teaching each year is when I get to introduce the book *Hatchet* by Gary Paulsen. *Hatchet* is about a teenage boy who survives a plane crash in the Canadian wilderness. Brian, the main character, sits down and cries because he is cold, hungry, tired, and lost in the woods. When he is finished crying he is still cold, hungry, tired, and lost in the woods. My interpretation that I discuss with my students is that Brian comes to realize that his old teacher, Mr. Perpich, was right when he once suggested that Brian has to take positive steps to make his life better. Otherwise, nothing is going to change. "You are your best asset," Perpich says. Brian applies this same philosophy to life in the woods – survival depends on actually doing something to make the situation livable.

When David was first diagnosed with cancer I wrote a letter to my students explaining why I wasn't going to be in school for a while. I told them that I was dealing with my own "Mr. Perpich moment." They all knew exactly what I was talking about. They understood that I was in a tough spot and I felt like I had to do something – anything – to make my family's situation better. Even small steps, such as writing a journal every time something came up, felt very important to me. I had to keep moving.

Thinker Dad is the guy who has to pull back for a while. It is possible that Thinker Dad has been stunned into inactivity by the news of his child's illness. However, I believe Thinker Dad is like a duck on a pond. On the surface he's calm and collected. Underneath he's paddling like crazy. He has to think about things and deal with the issues and emotions internally before he can take any action. Thinker Dad doesn't mind periods of inactivity. He is conserving his energy for those moments when his actions will do the most good.

Thinker Dad probably thinks Action Dad is a bit of a jerk who likes to run around like a chicken with its head cut off, wasting time on little things that don't really matter. Action Dad probably thinks Thinker Dad is a bit of a mamby-pamby who won't get off his duff to get anything done.

Even though I am probably an Action Dad, I'm not saying one is better than the other. They are just different sides of the same coin. Any dad is going to feel a flood of different emotions during those first few days, anger, grief, confusion, fear, etc., and every dad has different ways of dealing with those emotions.

It doesn't matter if you are the type to jump up and do something or if you are more pensive and thoughtful. You might even be somewhere in between, and I might have to add a third category of dad: Just Plain Dad. (Please note: after talking with plenty of parents while researching this book, I've decided that Action Mom and Thinker Mom are also appropriate designations.

However, being an Action Dad, I'm kind of stubborn and I'm not about to change these designations because of simple male/female issues. I have to assume that this information is valid regardless of gender.)

Dr. Kurt Soell, a psychologist and psychotherapist in St. Louis who works with support groups for patients and their families, agrees with the general principle of Action Dad versus Thinker Dad (and how it doesn't have to be just dads).

"I don't see it with just dads, but as males we are definitely fixers," he said. "Some parents want as much information as possible right now. Others want to know just what (they) need to know right now. This is both male and female."

Regardless of how you handle things, you have to remember that this time isn't about you. This time is all about your child and making sure he or she gets through this situation with as little fuss as possible. This is especially true for older children. Children who are old enough to at least partially understand what's going on will be looking to you to see how they should react. If you freak out, then they probably will too. If you stay calm, and even Action Dad can have calm activity, then it will help alleviate your child's fears and help them get through this.

If you absolutely must freak out, then you absolutely must do it somewhere away from your child. When the time is right, leave the room for a minute. Make up an excuse to get away before you break down. I found that the hospital's chapel was a good place for me to have my little depressed fits, not because I'm all that religious.

Strangely, the chapel was always deserted so I felt like I could have some privacy there.

When David was sick, he was our only child. Add that to the fact that he was still very young, too young to have school plans or social activities, and we had a much easier time of it than many parents. Families with more than one child, especially if they have older children, have an extra burden during the first few weeks and throughout the treatment process, they have to keep their families together and corral the attitudes and concerns of their entire group. We never had to deal with hurt feelings because a basketball game was skipped in favor of a doctor visit. We also never had to deal with siblings feeling scared or jealous of the attention we were giving David. Many families are not in that position.

Being open and honest with the entire family will help alleviate some of that stress. No, you don't need to tell everyone absolutely everything. Be cognizant of age-appropriate discussions, but come on. You know your children are smart enough to figure out that something big is happening. You might leave the room to make a phone call or you might hold whispered conversations in the hallway. They can see that you've been crying but you tell them nothing is wrong. All that will do is make them sure that you are keeping secrets. It will damage their trust in you and probably make them even more nervous when the truth finally does come out.

Amy Kennedy is a child life specialist at St. Jude. She works with the children and their families to make sure everyone is adjusting to their new situation and their new surroundings. She said older children, especially teens, can be very adept at figuring out the truth. They may not know specific details, but they can tell that something serious is happening. This is true for initial diagnosis all the way through the final outcome of the disease.

"A lot of times they are waiting for their parents to say it is okay (to talk about cancer). They are worried about their parents," Kennedy said. "They are stronger than we give them credit for."

Once you've shared the news, you should be certain the entire family is ready for some changes and some challenges. Siblings should know that they are important but that they might have to make some sacrifices for the sake of their sick brother or sister. Assure them that, whenever possible, their activities and interests will be as much of a priority as they were before the diagnosis.

"While (siblings) are not going through this physically, it is just as hard on them emotionally," Kennedy warned.

If children know what's going on they should be allowed to ask questions. The freedom to ask questions will ease a lot of the burdens on them. Unspoken concerns may seem like secrets to a child and can be a source of stress. You might not always have an answer to their questions, or maybe not an answer they want to hear, but they should feel free to ask.

It will probably help if you try to anticipate the possible questions from your children. Plan out some answers ahead of time, especially for the big questions, such as "Am I going to die?" "What happens if I die?" etc. These questions can and probably will come up, especially with older children. Be ready for them. Your child is watching for what you say and how you say it. You don't necessarily have to have a "yes" or "no" answer. In some cases answers like, "We're doing everything we can to avoid that" can be good enough, especially if you sound confident when you respond. Practice helps.

Don't be afraid to ask for help. Counselors, social workers, clergy, and your doctors all have experience with these kinds of question. Talk to them about your child and your family. Ask for their advice.

Culpepper said parents need to understand that everything will be different. It doesn't have to be bad, but it will not be the same. Flexibility will have to be your new watchword. Plans can and will change because of your child's illness. Nothing relating to your child's health can be considered simple any more. A mild fever to most children is an annoyance, but to a child with cancer a fever could easily end in a trip to the emergency room. Nothing is going to come before your child's health, not vacations, trips to grandma's house, anniversaries, or graduations. Nothing will be more important.

"You have to drop the idea that you are ever going to have a normal life," she said. "My biggest struggle that first six weeks was that I tried to make their lives normal. There is nothing normal about this time. When I let go of that, about six weeks in, it was a huge burden that was lifted."

This does not mean it is acceptable to go overboard. Your children will be looking to you to see what their reactions should be. This is especially true for younger children. If you fall to pieces, they will fall to pieces too. If you are confident, calm and secure, your children will echo these emotions.

Be aware of pitfalls. Do not let the old rules and standards of behavior go out the window just because of a diagnosis. Make an effort to maintain the same boundaries and expectations for your children. They are resilient and they can handle the changes, probably better than you can, but they have to maintain some sense of normality. Also, bad behavior can be a hard habit to break once things calm down. Of course your child may act out. That's often how children respond to stress. Are you going to let them get away with it? No. Would you let your child's personality change because of the flu? Sure, the circumstance is different, but only because of the scale. A child's behavior is their behavior – it isn't the disease. You wouldn't let your child's behavior go south because they had the flu. Don't let them become someone they're not because of cancer or some other serious illness.

Kennedy said it can be a challenge for parents to set boundaries for their children in a hospital, especially when grandparents, friends, aunts, uncles, and everyone else visits and seems to want to treat the child like royalty.

"In a hospital environment, everyone wants to give you things," she said. "It's okay to say, 'No.' It's okay to set limits. Know that your children are going to test those limits. That's what children do."

Kennedy said hospital visits, especially if the child is feeling good, can almost seem like a visit to grandma's house or a day with a substitute teacher. The rules may seem like they are different because of the different situation. As a parent, it is your job to reinforce the behaviors you think are important. Children like to know where they stand. Things feel normal to them when the normal rules are enforced in the normal ways. It is like a security blanket. If nothing else, you should plan for your child's future once the hospital visits are over. Do you really want to live with the spoiled child you've created if you're lax in your expectations?

"Your kid could be well, but nobody is going to want to be around them," Culpepper joked.

It will certainly sound odd, but you have to think about yourself during this time too. You won't be any use to your child or the rest of your family if you allow yourself to burn out during this stressful time. Of course, taking a long vacation right now is out of the question, but finding an hour or two for yourself once or twice a week is a great idea. You can recharge your mental and emotional batteries and be ready for whatever else comes next.

This same advice holds true for your marriage. It is too easy for couples to lose track of each other during this time. Protect your marriage by making time to be a couple. One of David's first nurses made certain that Rachel and I left the hospital. She practically kicked us out during one of David's naps. She also gave us very strict instructions that we were to go to a restaurant she knew of down the street from the hospital, and we were not allowed to come back for two hours. Who am I to go against sound medical advice like this?

Later on, when friends and family asked what they could do to help, we usually suggested that they pick up gift cards to that restaurant. I don't think they realized how important those cards, and the meals away from the hospital the cards represented, were to us. They gave us a little taste of normal life, an all-too rare taste that was treasured.

Most hospitals will have a social worker, or someone in a similar position, stop by for a brief consultation fairly soon after an initial diagnosis. Don't worry. This is normal. The nurses don't think you are a nut who needs special handling. Most hospitals do this as a matter of routine. These specialists are there to help you as you adjust to your new role as a caregiver and the parent of a child with cancer.

They are probably going to ask some questions that seem like they are a little too personal and/or have nothing to do with your child's case. They might ask about recent life events, such as deaths or other illnesses in the family, job changes, housing moves, that kind of thing. They are looking for patterns and how you have dealt with other stress-inducing situations.

Judith Hicks, a licensed clinical social worker at St. Jude, said people in her position take a broad view of the family.

"We look to see how they function prior to the diagnosis. The diagnosis of a catastrophic illness alone is enough to upset the balances of a family," she said. "This is a huge crisis for any family. It shakes the foundations. It shakes your sense of life being safe and fair. How can this happen to a child?"

Families who have dealt with life-changing events in the past might fall back into old patterns – some good, some not so good. For example, if you've faced a death in the family and were able to rally support and grieve in a healthy way, it is likely you will be able to adjust to your new circumstance in a positive way.

However, if you have a history of falling apart during a crisis, the social worker will be able to coach you through this new reality with some helpful guidance. The social worker at the hospital will likely stay with a family throughout the family's entire association with the hospital – initial diagnosis, treatment, remission, relapse, release, etc. The social worker's job will be to continually assess how you are handling your situation and, if necessary, they can recommend steps.

I wish I'd spent more time with the social workers at SLCH. Like a lot of Action Dads, I guess I thought I could shake off any injury or stress without any help. I ignored their offers to help, and I was wrong. Early intervention could have saved me a lot of unnecessary heartache. Eventually, I did start seeing a private therapist, but I wonder if maybe I could have avoided that problem, and expense, if I'd done the right thing and listened to the social worker early on.

Hicks said grief isn't just for parents who lose a child. If you are getting a serious diagnosis for your child, regardless of what the projected outcomes are going to be, you are going to experience some level of grief. If nothing else, you will grieve your loss of innocence and the loss of the life you thought your child was going to have. Even if your child successfully completes treatment and has a strong remission, there will always be a nagging doubt in the back of your mind, a "what if ..." that doesn't go away.

"There is a grief in the beginning, the loss of a healthy child and the dreams we have for them," Hicks explained.

Even now that they are veterans of this kind of situation, both Lambert and Culpepper say they get those "what if" moments in their heads now and then.

"I wonder, was it something I did (that caused the cancer)? Was it something in the house? I still worry about everything. We don't spray the yard for fear that it could cause problems," Lambert said.

Culpepper agreed. "There is a loss of innocence. Once you've taken that path you can't go back."

Finally, Hicks suggests taking a "Right Now" approach. Look at what you need to get through your situation right now, then later you can look for deeper strategies for the long-term. Sometimes an initial diagnosis is too big to deal with. Take those situations day-by-day until you are ready to move out of crisis management mode and into a more stable way of coping.

Both Action Dad and Thinker Dad have the same problem right now. Regardless of which type of dad you are, doctors are telling you that there is something wrong and, chances are, they are not sure exactly what they are dealing with. Waiting for the pathologist reports can be the hardest thing, especially for Action Dad. It can take days, sometimes even weeks, before doctors can say for certain what they are dealing with. When we first went to St. Louis Children's Hospital we were told to pack for a four- to five-day stay. We were there for almost two weeks because David's cancer was so rare.

Don't worry that these first few days seem like they are a blur. The doctors, and everybody else associated with this part of the process understand what you are going through. They know they are going to have to repeat things several times during the next few days.

"Parents are not wired to know how to handle this," Dr. Soell said. "Oftentimes we want control and that's a healthy thing. When we hear a diagnosis of cancer, we want control and there is too much going on that we can't control."

Dr. Soell likened the situation to a fire drill. Since we were children we've had fire drills in school so we could know what to do if the real thing happens. We have practiced and we understand what we should do if a fire breaks out. There is no way to practice for cancer, no way to prepare yourself for what a diagnosis brings into your life.

"It is all about getting perspective. Some (parents) can do it quickly but with others it can take some time," Dr. Soell explained.

I know in our situation, our doctors, nurses and other hospital personnel probably gave us the same information at least three times. They also gave it to my wife's parents, my sister, several of our friends, and coworkers. I wouldn't be surprised to find that during that first week they had repeated some of the same information more than twenty times to different people, about half of those times were to me personally.

"(Parents) don't really remember those first few days. There is a lot of shock which is why we do a lot of explaining and talking with families. We realize during those first few days we'll be repeating ourselves a lot," Dr. McDonald said. "You are only going to hear a portion of it based on the fact that you are in such a state of shock. We are really accustomed to having questions asked multiple times. A lot of times it's from the same family member or sometimes it's from a new family member showing up and the parents can't answer their questions. Because the new family member comes in and says, 'What is it?' and the parent is, 'Oh, they said something like …' We have to come back and explain again. It's part of the job."

Lambert, maybe an Action Mom, said she kept a different kind of journal during those first few days and weeks of her son's cancer as a way to help with the information overload. She made charts of exactly which medications her son was taking and their side effects. She kept track of the data so she was armed with information whenever she talked to his doctors. Essentially, Lambert became as much of an expert as she could so that she'd be ready for whatever came next.

Dr. Ross W. Shepherd is one of the country's leading experts on kidney and liver transplants. We were lucky enough to have him as the head of our transplant team at St. Louis Children's Hospital. He says most parents tend to have the same basic conversation with their doctors when they learn that their child is facing a serious illness that will probably require surgery or other drastic measures. Parents ultimately ask the same questions.

"The big one is really, 'Is this going to work? What are the chances? What are the risks?' Using such a desperate approach to this disease (such as surgery) must mean that there are serious risks involved. Usually the bottom line is that people want to know the truth," he said.

"People want to know what the end is going to be. They get to that in different ways. Sometimes they are in such shock that they can't deal with it yet. You (as the doctor) have to give them a little bit of time to come to terms with it, but that's the bottom line. Is it going to work? All of the other details that it is ultimately necessary to work through, all of the steps they go through to get a transplant pale into insignificance when compared to the big question: Is this going to work?"

Dr. Dreyer agrees. She said other big-ticket questions include how the treatment, especially if it involves radiation, will effect the child's ability to have children of their own some day. Parents often also worry about how the child's growth will be affected, how their appearance could change, or if the treatments might cause developmental delays or other problems in school.

"The obvious question is, 'Will my child survive?' after that parents want to know if they will be able to function normally in life," Dreyer said.

Parents shouldn't be afraid to ask questions of their doctors. Go ahead, ask what this means for the child's future.

I remember when we were first told about David needing to have a liver transplant I asked several questions about what the surgery would mean for his future athletic prospects. Could he play football in high school? When I learned that the answer was "No," I was disappointed. Now, keep in mind, I'm not a sports guy. I doubt that my child would really want to play football if he didn't grow up in a house where we watched sports on television or read the sports page before the front page, but it could happen, and I was concerned about that.

I was actually disappointed to learn that David didn't have a chance to become an MMA champion in the Octagon. I'd thought about signing him up for karate or tae-kwon-do lessons as a way to keep him physically fit and to give him a bit of self-confidence. If the class led to him beating someone into submission in the Octagon as a way to make a living, so be it.

So anyway, sports questions were my goofy questions. Yours might have something to do with their odds of becoming an award winning saxophone player or if they are going to have scars that show when they put on a prom dress. It doesn't matter what your concerns are or how trivial they may seem to others. Ask those questions and make sure you receive answers. Sure, they may not be the answers you want but at least you will know. You don't need anything else on your mind that might keep you up at night worrying or wondering. Trust me. You will have plenty of other things keeping you awake.

Remember, worry and doubt are part of the process. Knowing

this doesn't make it any easier to deal with worry and doubt, but it might make you understand that you're not going crazy, which is important too.

Dr. McDonald says there should not be any medical questions that go unasked or unanswered. It is the doctors' responsibility to make certain you understand all of the important need-to-know information. It is your job to make sure you get answers to the want-to-know questions.

If you get home and realize that you forgot to ask an important medical question (or, more likely, you simply forgot the answer to that important medical question) don't worry. Most hospitals, especially those that are large enough to handle the kinds of problems you are facing, probably have a 24-hour hotline you can call.

Don't expect that the doctor you want to talk with will be the one answering the phone. It is rare that a doctor will give out his or her cell phone number to patients. Instead, you will probably reach the hospital's central operator. This person will page the on-call doctor for your particular problems, oncology, transplants, etc.

Different hospitals have different procedures for handling hotline calls but most feature doctors returning a phone call rather than have patients/parents on hold for long periods of time. One hospital we dealt with had a policy that the on-call doctor would begin returning phone calls every hour at the top of the hour. Another hospital had a policy whereby an on-call doctor would call you back within a certain time limit. Our usual wait was something like ten to twenty minutes before we spoke with the doctor. Often, if the question was general enough, the doctor could give us an answer right away. Usually, however, our questions were pretty specific so the doctor would have to call back again in a few minutes after he or she had checked David's records.

Apart from the wait time calling a hospital hotline can be a tricky situation. I had quite a few "Do I call/Don't I call?" moments. Finally, I decided that I would call anytime I had a question. This is my son we're talking about and I didn't really care if I sounded like a goof for asking a dumb question. In this situation there are no dumb questions. There are good questions and there are the questions you wish you had asked.

The hotline call is perfect for those, "Huh, I forget. Should he be eating dairy products, or will that make him nauseous with his new medication?" type questions. The hotline is also a good resource for those moments when you need to confirm your doctor's orders regarding home healthcare.

The first call like this I had to make with David came when we started giving him medication through his chest tube by ourselves. The home health care nurse thought the medicine should be given in a certain way and at a higher dosage. Her way, however, didn't quite gel with what I remembered the doctors telling us. One hotline call later and the nurse was doing things my way.

I tried not to gloat, but I didn't try very hard. (Side note: this was the same home healthcare nurse who later left an uncapped hypodermic needle in David's crib. Action Dad didn't take that very well and I made sure she never set foot in our house again.)

If you think something is seriously wrong with your child and he or she is in immediate danger, do not call the hotline. Call an ambulance or go to the emergency room. If you feel like you have to make a phone call during this time, call ahead to the emergency room to let them know you are on the way and that your child has a special situation. This can cut your wait time, and it gives the hospital staff time to get things ready for you. They might even end up calling your child's doctor to get specific information about your child's needs.

If, on the drive over to the hospital, you still have the desire to use the phone you might want to call your insurance company. They like to know when their clients are about to run up a big emergency room bill so they can start the paperwork early. Some insurance companies even require pre-admission notice before they are willing to pay for an emergency room visit. Check with your provider to see what their specific policies are.

The Second Opinion

When we first started telling people about David's cancer most of them went immediately to one place, the second opinion. "Did you get a second opinion?" I've answered this question with both "yes" and "no," and it seems that, depending on who is asking the question, you could be wrong either way.

If you say that you haven't gone for a second opinion, it seems that people will judge you as being an uncaring parent. How dare you not get more advice when your child's life is on the line? That sounds reasonable, right? Wrong, because people will also judge you if you say you have gotten a second opinion. Yeah, it's true. It seems that by asking for (and receiving) a second opinion you just confirmed their fears that your doctor is a moron who couldn't diagnose his/her way out of a wet paper bag. How dare you stick with this idiot when you clearly do not trust them with your child's life?

You can't win when someone asks you about getting a second opinion. I think the best response is that you are looking at all of the options. Then don't answer any more of their questions on the subject. It's not their job to second guess you and frankly, it isn't any of their business anyway.

"These people are seagulls," said Dr. Justin N. Baker, the director of the Hematology/Oncology Fellowship Program at St. Jude Children's Research Hospital. "They make a lot of noise and a lot of mess and they cause families to question what they are doing.

Once things calm down, they fly away (without providing any real help)."

The second opinion question has probably already happened to you or you may have had this thought on your own. While it is healthy to have a bit of skepticism about a diagnosis, too much skepticism can be a dangerous waste of time. In most cases there isn't a huge rush but, if it looks like it is going to take more than a couple of days to get a second (or third) opinion, don't bother. You probably don't have that much time.

When David was diagnosed Dr. Shepherd told us about the chemotherapy and surgical protocols they would be using. He mentioned how St. Jude Children's Research Hospital in Memphis, Tennessee has had some success using such-and-such technique. I don't remember the specifics (trust me, this kind of memory lapse will happen to you too especially when doctors are using medical terms with way more syllables than you are used to hearing) but I keyed in on the fact that he mentioned St. Jude.

Thinking back, I was probably a bit rude. I interrupted him and said something like, "If St. Jude is so good, shouldn't we be heading down to Memphis for the rest of the treatment?" At the time, I didn't know how much of a big deal Dr. Shepherd was, but my rudeness didn't phase him at all. He'd probably heard that same question from at least half of the patients he dealt with that day. After all, St. Jude is another nationally recognized hospital that specializes in children's cancer.

It turns out that, he'd already been in touch with doctors at St.

Jude. In cases with life threatening issues (cancer, transplants, etc.) the doctor giving you the news is probably part of a team of doctors who have studied the case. In David's case, we had a team of general physicians, an oncology team and a transplant team (probably more than a dozen doctors overall) reviewing David's file, reaching a consensus, checking with colleagues in other hospitals, and looking out for his best interest before they ever talked to us.

Even with all of those doctors (not to mention their support staffs, nurses, pathologists, radiologists, etc. all of whom have experience with these matters) Dr. McDonald still turned to a doctor on the East Coast who specializes in rhabdoid tumors to confirm the diagnosis and the treatment protocols.

Sometimes you hear about doctors having a God complex, but it is an understandable condition for them, especially if they are one of the top guys like Dr. Shepherd. They make life-and-death decisions all the time and, if they are good at what they are doing, they make the right call. How can that not give someone a big head, right?

In the movie *Malice*, Alec Baldwin plays a prominent surgeon who is being interviewed at a deposition about some procedure he handled. He has a great line: "If you are looking for God, he was in operating room number two on November 17 and he doesn't like to be second guessed. You ask me if I have a God complex? Let me tell you something, I am God."

Well, great line from a movie aside, I found out how wrong the whole God complex theory can be when it comes to a serious case.

When the doctors at SLCH couldn't find out what was wrong with David, their egos took a distant back seat to his health. They made the calls for help.

Baker said doctors a generation or two ago might have had a problem with requests for second opinions – maybe that's where the idea got started – but that kind of attitude has been left in the distant past.

"Gone are the cowboy days of, 'I'm the physician and I know best,'" he said, adding that a team approach for diagnosis, protocols, furthering treatment, etc. is the most common approach for todays doctors, regardless of their particular field or discipline.

If, after all that, you still don't feel comfortable and want to get your own second opinion, go for it. Ask your doctor about finding a second opinion and trust that they are not going to send you to someone who isn't qualified. They won't send you to someone just because they know that doctor will agree with them. In fact, they may want someone to disagree with them because the other doctor might find something they missed. They really do want what's best for your child, and they aren't going to let their ego get in the way of saving a life.

One thing I'd suggest is that you don't bother searching the Internet for answers. There are way too many kooks out there who don't know what they are talking about. Unfortunately, those kooks may seem like they have all the answers at a time when you are desperate for some kind of hope.

If you've seen the movie *Lorenzo's Oil* or any one of a hundred different made-for-TV-movies on Lifetime, you have seen stories about parents who found a miracle cure just in time to save their child. Watching these movies it is easy to believe that any idiot off the street can do a better job of treating your child's disease than the doctors can. Don't believe the hype. Just because some dude in Eastern Europe claims to be doing wonderful things with lasers these days doesn't make it true.

Please don't pin your hopes on some experimental treatment that hasn't been tested by the FDA. Herbal remedies, acupuncture, and yoga are great and they can be a big help, especially if using those products or procedures makes you or your child feel better and gives you hope. Don't get me wrong. I'm a fan of some of those things, Rachel is a 15-year yoga fanatic and occasional yoga teacher, but you are never going to cure cancer with a cup of tea, a needle, and some stretching. It simply isn't going to happen.

The Care and Feeding Of Your Hospital Staff

"Nurses are the heart of healthcare."

-Donna Wilk Cardillo

A Daybook for Beginning Nurses

It may seem strange to people who are not familiar with hospitals, but there are certain things you should do when you deal with hospital staff – doctors, nurses, aides, cafeteria workers, custodians, and everybody else. You should treat them like people.

Gasp! Shock! Awe!

Yeah, it's that simple. Show them the same respect that you would show any other professional. Never mind that these particular professionals hold your child's life in their hands. No, wait. Scratch that. Keep that fact front and center in your mind. These particular professionals hold your child's life in their hands.

I'm not saying that rude patients get worse care. Not a chance. Remember, these people are professionals and many of them have even taken a sacred oath to do whatever they can to help their patients (there are times when I think that the Hippocratic and the Marine Corps Oaths are the only two that the vast majority of people actually adhere to). What I'm saying is that, if you are polite or maybe even nice, you may find yourself on the receiving end of a few perks or, at the very least, you might find that your hospital stay is a touch more pleasant.

We are living proof that this can happen. I'm not going to say which hospital it was, but one of the charge nurses at one of the hospitals really seemed to like Rachel. They didn't become best friends, but they were friendly and the charge nurse began to look out for us a bit. (If you don't know it yet, the charge nurse is the one who oversees the operations on the floor. Think of her as the office manager or head secretary at your job. She doesn't have the most glamorous title or the best pay in the building, but everything goes to Hell when she isn't around). When that particular charge nurse was on duty and knew we were coming in for any kind of overnight stay we always seemed to end up with a slightly better room, better view, bigger fold-out bed, quieter roommate, etc.

I fully believe that the extra nice treatment started out because of Rachel's relationship with the charge nurse. It couldn't have been because of anything I'd done. In fact, if we had been judged solely on my behavior, we probably would have ended up sharing the worst possible room on the floor (the one with the broken television and the fold-out bed with the uncomfortable, bad-smelling, and oddly stained mattress) with the worst possible roommate.

Our first day at St. Louis Children's Hospital, I was understandably nervous. David had only just been diagnosed recently, and I still wasn't comfortable spending time in hospitals (who is, right?). The nurse was doing her job, probably taking David's vitals or something, and David was a bit scared and cranky. During the course of handling her duties, the nurse let the side of the crib slide down onto David's foot, pinning him to the mattress. He wasn't hurt, just surprised and uncomfortable. He was already out of sorts because he wasn't at home and he'd been poked and prodded. Of course he screamed and, upon seeing what had happened, I screamed right along with him.

His screaming was simply loud. It did a good job of expressing his displeasure while remaining inarticulate (he was seven months old). My screaming, however, was loud and full of well thought out, fully articulated four-letter words about how that particular four-letter-word-ing nurse had better get her three-letter-word away from my son before I four-letter-word-ing did something I'd regret.

I want to go on the record publicly saying that my actions were inappropriate. Even though that nurse should not have let the side of the crib fall on David, I should not have lost my temper. A little while later, I walked down to the nurses station to make a public apology (thinking that the other nurses had probably heard me yelling) and, amazingly, she accepted my apology without any retaliation. She, and the other nurses, said it happens all the time (impulse control and temper control are probably two of the more negative traits of Action Dad) and that they understand how parents are under a lot of stress and sometimes don't need a lot of provocation to set them off.

Although my kind of bad behavior was fairly common among dads, the nurse said that apologies were much more elusive. Amazingly, she didn't hold my bad behavior against me or, more importantly, my son. However, showing just a smidge of extra respect for her by apologizing gave my reputation at the hospital a bit of a boost. Over the course of the next several months of David's treatment, that particular nurse became one of my favorites and eventually we laughed about my earlier bad behavior. She was one of the nurses who came in and cried with us when she heard that David's case had become terminal.

I said the good treatment we received started out because of Rachel's relationship with the charge nurse. I did not say we continued to get this treatment because of that single relationship. My beginning bad behavior aside, Rachel and I made conscious efforts to maintain good relationships with the hospital staffers. We tried our best not to be obnoxious or too picky. We didn't ring the call button to ask a nurse to bring us sodas (I'd heard of that happening. I imagine that guy slept on the funky couch during his next visit).

I even took a bit of advice from a friend who had spent a lot of time in a hospital with one of her sons. She said there were three ways to get on the good side of an overworked, underpaid, and under-appreciated nurse.

First: Maintain a pleasant, positive attitude, as much as possible, under the circumstances.

Next: Show genuine appreciation for their efforts on your behalf. It's amazing what saying "thank you" and really meaning it will do.

Lastly: Give them chocolate.

Yep, that last one is probably playing dirty but I don't care. I took an extra paper bowl from the cafeteria's salad bar and filled it with several different kinds of candy from the hospital gift shop. I put the bowl on the counter next to the sink. The nurses and aides all have to wash their hands before and after every visit and the custodians always clean up around there, so I knew everyone would see it. I put up a small sign which read, "If you are helping David, help yourself to a treat. You are appreciated."

I made sure that I kept the bowl full and even asked around to see what their favorite candies were (chocolate seemed to win in most cases). Sure, we had a few extra nurses or aides dropping by now and then for a little pick-me-up but it was worth it.

By the end of that week, all of the nurses on the floor knew who we were and they were glad we were there (well, not glad we had to be in a hospital, but you know what I mean). They smiled at us in the hallway, and we always had a good room with a non-funky couch. They stopped by to celebrate any good news we had with David's treatment and they were extra quiet when they had to take David's vitals in the middle of the night. Believe me, a quiet night nurse is a God-send. It's hard enough to fall asleep in a hospital without having loud nurses bang around at Oh-Dark-Thirty in the morning.

What's more, and this may be a coincidence but I doubt it, we were always the last family on the floor to have a roommate when space got tight. You can't buy that kind of treatment … oh, wait. Yes, you can. All it costs is a little courtesy and about $10 worth of mini Reese's Peanut Butter Cups, mini Hershey Bars and some little packs of Twizzlers.

I've heard that nurses are drawn to their special fields

(pediatric, oncology, surgery, etc.) because of their personalities and that pediatric nurses tend to be more fun-loving, whimsical, or even childlike because they deal with children. I see the same kind of behavior in schools with different teachers drawn to different grades or different curriculum areas (compare your third-grade teacher, your junior high art teacher, your driver's ed. teacher, and your calculus teacher and you'll know what I'm talking about).

Regardless of why they were drawn to their particular field, be thankful that you have the nurses you have – especially if you can connect with them on a personal basis.

I feel bad that I didn't interview some of David's nurses for this book. God knows, they deserve a lot of the credit for getting us through those hard days in the hospital. I'm just not sure I could face them again and maintain any façade of professionalism. I was able to put on my old reporter hat for a while and distance myself from the emotional content of the interviews with most of the people I've spoken to for this book. On the days I interviewed the doctors, social workers, and all types of coordinators, I managed to stop by for a quick visit with some of the nurses that helped us. It had to be a quick visit because the emotions that came flooding back when I saw those women threatened to overwhelm me.

When things were darkest, they cried right along with me. I guess that's the most important thing I can say about them. Heck, I'm sitting at my computer trying not to get choked up just remembering them.

I've left discussing the care and treatment of doctors for last for a reason. Doctors are a different breed of hospital staffer. While they are ultimately in charge of your child's care, you won't be dealing with them in the same up close and personal way that you deal with the nurses and the nurses' aides. Most people, I assume, naturally treat doctors with a little more respect and courtesy than they treat the other hospital employees. Theirs is a universally esteemed profession for a reason.

I think it is worth noting here that doctors, for all of their training and professionalism, are people too. They have the same feelings as everyone else. Through necessity, they have usually learned how to keep those emotions in check while they are on duty. Do not think for a moment, however, that they don't care and that they don't become emotionally attached to their patients and their patients' families.

Dr. McDonald said all doctors, regardless of their number of years in the profession, have to feel certain things when they go into a room to tell a family that a child has cancer or that a child has very limited time left.

"It's a very different mindset when I have to go in to tell a family that it is a cancer with a 15 percent cure rate. There is likely nothing we can do. A lot of what goes through my head in that moment is the same grieving process (as the child's family and friends), especially when I've met the kid and their families and I get to know them. I have to internalize a lot of it, but it is the how or why that (the family) feels. This is a cute kid in there playing and having fun, and I know as a doctor that there is a good chance that he won't be here six months from now," she said. "You have to put that aside when you walk in that room because it's not about you. It's about that family and what they need. With you (in David's case) I sat in the back room. I allowed myself a few tears. I cried a little bit, then I got myself together. I had done the research. I had tried to find everything I could find. I'd talked to everyone I could talk to. I tried as hard as I could to find something we could do.

"It's very difficult as a doctor to go in a room and tell someone that you can't do anything else. One of the struggles as a doctor is to not feel like a failure when that happens, but you do. A little part of you feels like you failed that child and that family. Intellectually and mentally, you know you did everything. Every doctor goes through it differently, but it is always the worst thing to have to do. Every time I do it, it is as hard as the first time. It never gets any easier."

Dr. Baker could possibly know more about this situation than anyone else. He oversees palliative care at St. Jude Children's Research Hospital. Relatively speaking, palliative care is to doctors what hospice care is to nurses. It deals with pain management, especially when it comes to end-of-life issues. There's a lot more to palliative than just working with terminally ill patients, but the analogy is as close as I can come. About 60 percent of all metropolitan hospitals have a specialist like Baker on staff. This number could grow to close to 100 percent within about five years.

"I am put there for those families at their most difficult times to be a source of strength," he said. "I see what kind of doctor they need me to be. When I can meet those needs it is very fulfilling."

I'm sure many people would be surprised to learn that a doctor in this situation can maintain his emotional focus. Palliative care specialists often get called in on cases that have very low cure rates. This doesn't mean palliative care is a death sentence. The pain-management aspect of palliative care can benefit a wide variety of nonfatal diseases. Still, Baker said he would have dried up emotionally if he hadn't been able to reassess his definition of success. A cure and a long, happy life are unlikely for many patients who have progressed to palliative care, but there are other ways to measure success. For example, a child might not live long enough to graduate from junior high school, but he might live long enough and be healthy enough for a trip to Disney World with his family or a special ballgame with his father.

"If you are simply focusing on the goal of a cure, you could end up seeing all of this time as a failure," Baker said. "(As a palliative specialist), you celebrate what you can with these patients and you mourn when you have to. Even in the context of mourning things can be better because you were a part of it."

How Am I Going To Pay For All This?

It's a sad reality of the world today, but medical care for big problems costs big bucks. It's something parents have to be prepared for when they learn that their child has a serious illness.

Before Rachel and I had even had time to digest and understand our new situation and before we could really comprehend that David was going to need a major surgery and months, if not years, of intensive medical treatments, we were hit with the fact that we were going to have to pay for all of this somehow.

We knew we had insurance, but we didn't ever take the time to really review what it would cover. We never thought we'd have to. Like most parents, we were concerned enough about our insurance to look at what our co-payments would have to be during routine doctor visits. We knew David's immunizations would be covered and that emergency room visits had decent coverage for if/when he jumped out of a tree or fell off his bike. We never really thought about big-ticket items on his insurance policy.

We had a hard wake-up call, and we learned that transplant surgeries are never cheap. There is no way around that fact. In normal circumstances, if there is such a thing with transplant surgeries, the cost can run anywhere from $200,000 on the low end all the way up to well more than $1 million on the high end for childhood transplants.

Kidneys are the most commonly transplanted organs and are,

for some reason, more readily available than other organs, possibly because living donors can get by with only one kidney. Kidney transplants are also one of the least expensive, averaging at around $200,000. David's liver transplant was going to cost about $425,000, again probably because living donors are possible here. Heart and lung transplants are the most expensive, averaging more than $1 million, sometimes considerably more depending on the condition of the patient.

Please keep in mind that these costs are just estimates. The actual price can vary greatly depending on the condition of the patient, and we all know that medical costs go up every year. Something else to keep in mind is the age of the patient. In general, younger patients increase the cost of transplant surgeries. This is especially true for newborns and infants. Surgical teams usually need costly extra training to work with the youngest patients.

There are also a number of variables with these patients that can also drive up the expense. For example, minor weight changes in an adult don't mean much, but a 30-pound child that gains or loses a pound or two can mean significant changes in medicine and anesthesia dosage. That kind of necessary precision can elevate the costs. Finally, there is a general shortage of available organs for patients this young which means the cost of finding and transporting donor organs will increase.

One of the biggest problems facing families looking for either a heart or lungs is that there are so few good donors available. Obviously, living donors are out of the question so that leaves only cadavers. The most common cause of death for otherwise healthy people is automobile accidents. Unfortunately, fatal auto accidents tend to leave victims with crushed chests, thus eliminating the possibility of heart or lung donations.

According to Susan Basile, the financial transplant coordinator that worked with us at SLCH, most hospitals have someone on staff who will talk to the parents about the costs associated with surgery and extended treatments, like chemotherapy, physical therapy, radiation treatments, and medicines, etc. This is especially true for all of the larger hospitals in the country that would be more likely to perform major transplant surgeries.

The financial transplant coordinator, or whatever their job title is at their specific hospital, sits down with the parents to look over their insurance information. It is their job, at least in the beginning while parents are still in a state of shock, to act as a liaison between the parents and the insurance companies. They check with the insurance companies to find out what the deductibles are on the policies. They also check to see what percent of the procedure is covered (some companies only cover part of the cost even after the deductible is met), what the maximum benefit coverage is, out-of-pocket maximums, etc.

We got really lucky. David was covered under Rachel's work insurance policy and her company had wonderful coverage. Our out-of-pocket maximum (the most we'd ever have to pay in a given year) was small enough that we'd met it within about a month and a half. We didn't have a maximum benefit. Most people are not so lucky.

Basile became our best friend when she walked into our room at the hospital and told us that we had very good insurance for David. She told us that she would deal with the insurance company for a while so we could concentrate on keeping our son healthy and ourselves sane.

"You've got too much on your plate already. That's what we're here for. We want to help the situation as much as possible," she said.

At first I thought we might have been a special case, but I found out later that the hospitals arrange for similar visits for most of their major cases. Do not be afraid to tell the financial coordinators to come back at a different time. They are there as a resource for you and most won't be offended if you ask them to give you a little space. Transplants, cancer, major illnesses or injuries all take quite a bit of time so the transplant coordinator can easily come back in a day or two when you are ready to talk. On most financial matters, a few days one way or the other won't really matter and frankly, who cares about money when you are worried about your child?

Before she had a chance to look at our insurance program, Basile told us that there are plenty of fund-raising options available for families, including several national transplant fund-raising organizations that exist solely to help in these exact situations. Be careful, however, to research the organization before you make any agreements. Be certain you are not signing up with a shady organization that does fund-raising in your name, but then keeps the majority of the money raised for itself.

Several people in our lives back at home offered to do fund-raising for us. The Parent Teacher Association at my school, the student council at my school, co-workers, friends, family members, and even community members who we'd never met all wanted to help out and most offered money.

There are some who stand out in my head as being extra special: The co-workers who donated well more than a thousand dollars, mostly in small bills, when they learned that David was sick; the students in my class who organized a walk-a-thon similar to their own version of the Relay for Life; the benefit skating party the PTA organized; the guys at the role-playing game shop who donated a percentage of their profits for a month; and the garage sale benefit put on by the other families at David's daycare are just a few examples.

We were blown away and, honestly, we felt a little guilty accepting that money when we knew David had good insurance coverage and that our out-of-pocket maximum was fairly small. We didn't want to hurt anyone's feelings by turning down their gifts, but I was fairly bothered by the amount of charity we were receiving. I have to admit, it was partly a pride thing but it was also the feeling that I was accepting money under false pretenses because we weren't struggling financially as much as many families in similar situations.

This nagged at me quite a bit until several people, usually close friends who were trying to give me more money, told me that they felt helpless when they were faced with David's cancer. They were sad and angry but, because they were not there with us to deal with the day-to-day steps and challenges, they felt even more impotent in this situation because they couldn't do anything positive to help other than make a donation. Of course, we spent some of that money. We needed to pay for meals and gas to and from the hospital, but we also forwarded a lot of that money on to the Ronald McDonald House in St. Louis.

Basile said that kind of attitude is common among friends, family, co-workers and community members. Rachel and I eventually learned to accept the donations with gratitude, knowing that everyone involved had the best intentions.

"When things happen like this, people want to help," Basile said. "Sometimes (donating money) is the only thing people feel they can do to help out."

I guess what it all comes down to is that people should not be afraid to look into their options, especially if their health insurance isn't quite up to par. In some cases, especially for families with little or no insurance, hospitals can work out arrangements for gradual repayment and some can even make adjustments to some of the costs. Again, the financial coordinator is your first and best resource here. Don't be afraid or ashamed to ask questions.

Hope

Despite the way it may seem now and then, "Hope" is not a four-letter-word. Well, technically it is, but it doesn't have to be.

I remember taking a class on Greek mythology when I was in college. During one lesson the conversation shifted around to Pandora's Box. According to the legend, Pandora was the most curious woman alive. She always had to know what was going on. She was given an ornate box by the gods and told that she should not open the box. Under no circumstances was it going to be okay for her to open the box. Hands off the box, Pandora!

Well, of course, curiosity eventually got the better of her and she opened the box. Mistake! By lifting the lid, Pandora allowed all of the evil things to escape their confinement. Prior to her, the world had been perfect and completely without evil. Yep, it is her fault that evil exists in the world today (sheesh, it's not like she ate an apple or anything. Right, Eve?). The story has a strange ending because, once all of the evil had escaped, Pandora looked in the box and saw one thing still inside – hope.

According to the professor, the moral of this story is that, even with all of the evil in the world, we still have hope to hold on to. Being the stubborn type, I had to argue a little bit. I remember speaking vehemently against the professor's idea that hope was such a good thing. I said hope belonged in the box with all the other evils in the world because hope was responsible for more suffering than anything else. When big hopes and dreams of greatness go unfulfilled it is a much bigger tragedy than simple failure.

Think about your favorite football team. The championship game comes down to the last few seconds of regulation play with your team in control of the ball, but trailing by a few points. A field goal isn't going to cut it. Hike! The ball is in the air, a perfect spiral. The star receiver is jumps up gracefully and, in what seems like slow motion, he misses the catch. Your team loses. Isn't that a more heartbreaking moment than if the team had been blown away from the very start of the game? That was my point about hope being a bad thing.

Oooohhhh, what a smart 19-year-old cynic I was.

Well, having been through a situation where hopes and dreams were left unfulfilled, I now have to rescind my earlier arguments and revise my position on hope. Yeah, it is easy to say something glib about how all prayers are answered and that, sometimes, the answer is "No," but that's weak. Without hope to hold on to, I wouldn't have made it through the darkest moments of David's treatments. Even though things didn't turn out like I'd hoped they would, I don't regret having hope.

Without hope, I never would have crossed off any of the items on my "Daddy To Do" list. Without hope, I probably never would have even created a "Daddy To Do" list in the first place. I never would have gotten to see David smile as he rode the carousel at the mall if I didn't have hope that this was just one of a lifetime of memories I was making. Without hope, I wouldn't have had the father-son talk in the backyard and I certainly wouldn't have taken

David to the zoo to be enthralled by the chicken (A FRICKIN'
CHICKEN!).

Dr. Shepherd says hope can be a valuable commodity for
patients and their families, especially when they are dealing with
serious, life-threatening illnesses or injuries.

"There are subtle things that go on within the concept of
fighting to beat a disease where that sort of pursuit does require a
real positive process," Shepherd said. "We actually do see that in
transplant patients where they are going to be cured by a transplant,
but they are waiting and waiting and waiting. In that circumstance,
fighting to stay alive to achieve that goal (of getting a transplant) is
important. The people who basically give up too early are the ones
who die too early."

One of the strange benefits of having an infant or very young
child going through a serious illness is that the child doesn't
understand the concept of giving up. Hope for tomorrow comes as
naturally to these children as breathing. He or she is going to keep on
being a kid and doing whatever kids do. Oh yeah, they may have to
do those things in a hospital and they won't like it when they feel bad
because of their treatments and they'll hate it when people come in to
stick them with needles, but they will keep on being kids and living
their lives. Seeing that spirit, that power of life winning through, is
enough to make even the most (pardon the pun) die-hard cynic think
twice.

"It's hard to be morose and depressed when your three-year-old
with Hodgkin's Disease is running around playing and being a kid,"

Dr. Dreyer said.

When David first went to SLCH, I hated walking through the hallways and seeing those sick kids. You know the kids I'm talking about, the pale, skinny, bald kids that were hooked up to IV drips or rolling slowly in unfamiliar wheelchairs. My first trip through that hall was depressing as hell.

Later on, though, I came to a different perspective. Because I'd seen David get pale, lose his hair, and drop weight, I learned to see past those things in those other kids. I stopped seeing poor, bald Taylor (the girl in the room next to ours who had leukemia) and I started to see Taylor, the fifth-grader who couldn't wait to get back to school. I saw Taylor, the little girl who wanted to have wheelchair races with her friends down the halls. I saw Taylor, the amazing, beautiful child who was doing everything she could to beat cancer because she didn't know any better. She was just a kid who happened to have cancer.

I rarely saw Taylor without a smile. Yeah, sometimes it was a tired smile or maybe even a forced smile, but she was smiling. She spent a lot of time in the hospital and it became a habit for me to check in on her whenever we took David down to St. Louis for a doctor visit. While David was sick, my students always wanted to get updates on her and she became a bit of an inspiration to them. If Taylor could do her homework with everything she was dealing with, my students knew they didn't have an excuse. I still talk about Taylor at least once a year with my students. I use her as an example of the power of a positive attitude. I'm pleased to say that, after hearing about Taylor, several of my students have made Locks of Love donations.

The last I heard, Taylor was heading toward remission and wasn't expected back in the hospital anytime soon.

Seeing the child behind the cancer is exactly the way to handle children with cancer. Dr. Shepherd warns parents against keeping children home from school or away from activities unless there is a valid, medical reason for doing so. Most parents eventually come to agree with him because they want their children to have full lives.

He said it is funny to him that some parents will keep a child home from school simply because the child may have a mild tummy ache but that same parent will fight to send a child with cancer to school because they don't want their child to miss out on anything childhood has to offer, including bullies, passing notes behind the teacher's back, school dances, and, yes, even homework.

"The idea of treating kids as kids, even if they have a serious disease, is important," Dr. Shepherd said. "Kids naturally don't want to be invalids. They don't know they (could) die tomorrow. They will do what they do and they will enjoy life right up to the very end. That's just the way they are."

Dr. Shepherd, however, also cautions against having too much hope or having unrealistic expectations. Sure, some parents are only going to hear what they want to hear when it comes to their child's prognosis (good or bad), but most parents are realistic enough to honestly hear what the doctors are saying. If they are paying attention, parents will know when the conversations shift away from treating the disease and start leaning toward making the patient as comfortable as possible while waiting for an inevitable end.

When Rachel and I received the news that David's cancer had spread, we were horrified. We went through a rush of emotions all at once that, unless you have been through that situation, are hard to understand. Once the shock of the news wore off, however, we were forced to take a hard look at our options. We didn't give up hope. Instead, we had to change what we were hoping for. Instead of hoping for a cure, we started to hope that David would have the best possible life for as long as possible. Unfortunately, quality of life and length of life are not the same thing.

There came a point in our conversation with Dr. McDonald and Dr. Shepherd when we realized we were talking about two different issues – quality and length. Ultimately, we decided to go for quality (this is where a palliative care doctor would typically step in). We wanted David to be happy and comfortable even if that meant we might lose him a month or two sooner. That might sound horrible, especially if you are reading this book as you are struggling with a similar situation. We knew we couldn't watch him waste away. We didn't want him to suffer because of our selfish need to have him with us for a few days longer.

Sure, if his prognosis was such that he could have undergone a radical or experimental treatment as a baby, but then live several years, we'd have been all about that. It would have been hard to watch as it was happening, but it would have been worth it to keep him with us for all that extra time. We knew, however, that he was going to die within a few months regardless of what we did. With aggressive, invasive, and painful treatment we might have kept him alive for a month or two longer, but no more than that. He would have suffered that whole time.

Dr. Shepherd says this type of decision is all too common for parents and, although he continues to struggle with what to say and how to say it, he usually counsels parents to err on the side of quality of life.

"There has to be some continuing, logical reason to keep on going with what you're doing. But then, eventually, there comes a point where that has to change and you have to say, 'This isn't working.' Most people who go through this process start to realize that, that's what they're dealing with. That's a bit of a shock. There comes a time when you are causing more harm than good. You are causing more pain," Shepherd said. "When you reach that point, you are causing harm unnecessarily. When you are in that circumstance, there is no way out."

This is where palliative care specialists, like Dr. Baker and Ms. Morgan, can be a Godsend for families. These doctors and specialists come up with the medically-based treatments that will keep the patient as comfortable and aware as possible, giving them the best hope for living a fulfilling life no matter how much of that life remains. The word many doctors use is "Re-goaling." Finding new achievable goals for the child and the family, goals that balance the medical reality with realistic hope.

"Without these goals (to work toward) they are not going to

recover as quickly," said Dr. Dreyer.

For example, goals might include returning to school for a while, hanging out with friends at a special place, or simply spending time at home again. Make-A-Wish Foundation dreams come into play here too.

"We are there to listen to what their goals are for themselves, their child and their families. We want to know what their hopes are," Morgan said. "We take time to hear their hopes and goals even if that means (we have to talk about) quality versus quantity of life."

These conversations can't help but be awkward. Everyone hates the idea that they might be giving up on a child, but that's the wrong way to look at this situation. You are not giving up on your child. In fact, you are giving that child the gift of the best life he or she can have.

"Hope has to be there. Hope is what sustains you. Hope is the lifeline, but hope changes," Baker said. "It shifts to these other things … going to the beach or not being in pain."

How Can I Help?

People always ask, "How can I help?" or they say, "Let me know if there is anything I can do ..." Of course, the biggest way they can help is by offering to help. You get it, right? Knowing that someone wants to help, that someone cares enough to put themselves out for your sake is usually a big boost. That moral support makes a difference.

This can be a lonely time. Don't be surprised if it feels like some people have abandoned you. In some cases, that might be true. Good riddance. In most cases, however, it is fear that keeps otherwise supportive people away. They don't always know how to say the right words or, more likely, they are really afraid of saying the wrong words. They are afraid that they will say something that might upset you. Basically, they don't want to make a bad situation worse.

People will tell you that situations like this will prove to you who your friends really are. I'm not sure if this is entirely true. It will show you who you can count on in a crisis, but I don't recommend throwing away a friendship just because you don't hear from someone every day.

You never know how your situation is effecting other people. Maybe they had a sibling with a serious illness when they were young. Maybe they simply get overwhelmed thinking about difficult circumstances.

"Friends might avoid you because they are afraid of saying the wrong thing. The support you thought would be there disappears. It can be very isolating for parents," Morgan said.

Still, there are going to be plenty of people who want to do something to show their support. My advice? Let them. They want to help and even if you don't want to admit it, you need help.

Dr. Soell has an acronym he uses with patients: S.T.A.R. It stands for Support, Tell, Acknowledge, and Respond.

Support: Getting help when you need it in the way that you need it.

"There are so many different levels of support – your spouse, your extended family, church, work. It is imperative to rally support," he said, adding that knowing when to seek support from a therapist, psychologist, or other professional is important too. "It's not a sign of weakness."

Tell: Be very specific when you ask for help. If you need someone to pick up a load of groceries you should ask for specifically that, as opposed to asking someone to "give you a hand sometime." Meals can be another example of specific help. When word of your child's diagnosis begins to spread, you will be inundated with offers for someone to cook meals for you. Find one trusted friend and make them the go-to person who will coordinate these meals. Otherwise you might find that you have 15 casseroles on your front porch the first day and no place to put them.

"Be specific. Say, 'Could you be in charge of _____'?" Dr. Soell said. "We don't want to sound needy and we want to save our favors for when we really need them. You really need them now."

Acknowledge: Be ready for a gamut of emotions to come at you when you aren't expecting them. Accept them for what they are and do not judge yourself too harshly. Do not feel guilty if you feel depressed or sullen. By the same token, don't feel guilty if you find yourself in a good mood now and then too. Life happens and, believe it or not, good moods can happen during cancer treatment.

"They feel like they need to be strong all the time," Dr. Soell said. "Parents aren't robots. They have to acknowledge their own feelings throughout the process (good and bad)."

He added that many times the depression we feel can be caused by fear. Asking questions and finding answers is the best way to combat that fear.

"When we talk about our fears, we tend to fear less. That 'What If?' moment can become huge (if left unexamined) or it can be dealt with and understood. We should focus on what we know rather than what might be. If we do that, fear becomes caution and proportionate."

Respond: This can be a bit tricky. Reacting is a gut instinct, emotional rather than rational. According to Dr. Soell, responding has an "extra filter" that comes into play. It's "taking information critically before taking action."

I like this. It appeals to the nerd in me in a Mr. Spock-like way. Taking logical action is difficult for Action Dads, but it is perfectly normal for Thinker Dads. Maybe there is a bit of Jedi calm in here too because fear and anger lead to the dark side of the Force. (Yeah,

I know I mixed Star Trek and Star Wars in the same paragraph. I'm going to lose nerd street cred for that).

One of our primary nurses (a Firefly and Babylon 5 Fan – just to continue the nerd theme) suggested that we find a national chain restaurant that is within easy walking distance to the hospital and ask people to give us a gift card to that restaurant. The fact that it is a national chain means that your friends can probably get the card without any real problem. The cards are available at Walmart and most major chain grocery stores. They can also order one on the internet.

Getting a card like that means you have to actually leave the hospital to redeem it. You are required to take a little time to yourself, time you can use to escape for a while and feel normal. St. Louis Children's Hospital had an Applebee's in a hotel that could be reached via skywalk from the hospital. That was great because we didn't have to go outside during the winter storms. I don't know how many Applebee's steaks I ate with mashed cauliflower and steamed broccoli. It became my "go-to" meal while in St. Louis.

Gas cards are another way people can help financially without handing you a wad of cash. Yeah, it sucks to admit it but travel costs mount up fairly quickly. A $20 gift card at a gas station can ease that burden a little bit. Normally, I don't like gift cards as a gift. It is too impersonal for my tastes, but this is different. This is about what you need and how they want to help. The gift giver gets to feel good about themselves because they helped and you get the benefit of an extra half a tank of gas. Win/win, right?

If someone offers to babysit you should accept it. Of course, it almost goes without saying that you should only accept this offer from someone you would trust with your child if he/she wasn't sick … duh!

An offer to babysit might mean that the person knows you well enough to know when you need a bit of a break, even if it is only a short break and even if you don't recognize the need in yourself. It could also mean that the person making the offer is a little short on funds (who isn't?) and this kind of service is the only thing they can afford. This is another win/win scenario. They get to feel like they did something special while you get to take a much needed break. This is one of those odd cases where the gift helps the giver as much as it helps the recipient.

Your friends and family love you, and they are hurting because you are hurting. They want to help you. For your sake and for theirs, let them.

A beautician friend might offer some help … let them cut your hair even if they only offered a vague suggestion that they wanted to do something. A masseuse can give you a neck/back rub (accept this gift!) or a mechanic might give your car a tune-up. I don't want to sound like a broken record, but these people who make offers usually really do want to help and it gives them a good feeling – possibly a feeling they want to continue to get by making additional offers to other people, maybe people who need the help more than you. Spread the good feelings and the help around. It is already too rare.

Don't take unfair advantage of them, but don't be afraid to accept their offers.

Morgan suggested that it can be a good idea to let your childrens' schools know what you are dealing with. No, you don't have to give them a full accounting of your diagnosis and treatment options, but it can "grease the wheels" a bit if the school administrators and the teachers know what is going on. The school will likely have counselors available if you need that service or if your child's siblings or best friends – along with their own school administrators – need a bit of help understanding what's going on.

"These teachers are on the front line with these children every day," Morgan said.

Even if they don't have children, teachers got into that profession because they care about kids. If they know your son/daughter is going through a crisis, they will take steps to help. The teachers and school administrators don't want to invade your privacy, but it might take a bit of stress off the family if the teacher knows why Bobby or Sally isn't turning in their homework. Often day-to-day assignments can be written off in most of these family crisis situations. Why stress out over a book report or a geometry lesson when there are far more important things to worry about?

Oddly, the opposite is also true. Sometimes the sick child wants nothing more than the normal routine of everyday school life. Homework, the once dreaded bane of their existence, can suddenly become a lifeline connecting them to the world they knew back home. And, let's face it, hospitals can be boring places. So dull, in fact, that having a little something extra do do, even homework, might be exactly what your child is looking for.

Letting school officials know the situation also lets them know what information to reveal to your child's friends and the friends' parents – or what NOT to reveal. The rumor mill tends to run wild at schools during family crisis times. We were lucky. David's Godparents were teachers at my school. Most of our closest friends were my coworkers. They were kept in-the-know and they were able to distribute accurate and appropriate information.

There is a web of support built into the school system. Take advantage of that support from social workers, counselors, child life experts, etc. that are already in place at the school. It will make your life easier. Of course, I'm biased. I'm a teacher.

Financial support is another way people like to help out. It's odd to say, but there are going to be times when people are almost throwing money at you. The local lodge or the school PTA might hold a fund-raiser in your honor. Yeah, it may sound strange but it might be possible that you do not need the money. Maybe you have really good insurance or maybe you have a wealthy grandparent who will cover the costs. Regardless, you will accept the money graciously from these fundraisers because it might be the only way the people who love you have of showing their support and you will not throw that back in their faces.

You can always donate the money to organizations that help people in your situation (Ronald McDonald House, Target House, Caring Bridge, etc.) if you don't need the money yourself. Again, this is as much about the people who are trying to help as it is about your need for help.

I guess what I'm trying to say here is that you should let your friends and family members make their gestures. If nothing else, do it because their gestures are important to them. Maybe this single act of generosity sparks something in them that leads them to become better people. Friends of mine recently told me that David's illness was their first chance to give to someone else. Since then they've created their own local charity to help our community. You never know how much good one good deed can do.

We always ask, "Why did this happen?" We want to find meaning in our trials. Maybe – and I am really stretching here, so bear with me – maybe the reason this cancer happened is because it will make someone else take positive steps that will impact other lives. Maybe your child's cancer will have an influence on someone who will use the situation as the inspiration for a much larger effort. Former students of mine have told me that they went into medicine and nursing partially because of David's illness.

We're all struggling to find meanings and reasons. Maybe this is one of those situations where God says, "Shut up and trust me. It sucks, but I know what I'm doing." I hope so.

Be warned. Some people sincerely want to help you, but other people seem to think they are buying tickets for a show. They have made their donation and now they feel entitled to learn the details of your child's disease and how you are coping. Clearly, I wrote this book and I kept a very public journal so I didn't mind if everyone knew what was going on. You might be a more private person and there is nothing wrong with that. You deserve your privacy. Don't let them bully you into revealing too much. I suggest you gather a set of stock phrases for people like this. "We're doing as well as can be expected, but I don't really want to talk about it," is one that works fairly well.

Faith

"They say God never gives you more than you can handle.
God must think I'm a badass."
– Author unknown

Okay, if you've read this book in its entirety, or if you've only read pieces, you have probably figured out that I'm not sure where I stand on faith. I haven't talked about it much because it can be a difficult situation. What is the advice people give about how to make friends ... never talk about religion, race, or politics? Yeah, that's me.

I attended Catholic schools when growing up. My father and my grandfather, men who are my role-models in so much of my life, were lay ministers at our church and heavily involved in their faith. I even attended a Catholic university when I went back to school to become a teacher. On paper, I should be a very religious fella. My faith was tested with David's illness and I'm not entirely sure if I passed that test.

Maybe you've already noticed, but people often want to ascribe some sort of extra wisdom to you when you've had a child with a serious illness or, as in my case, a child who died. Somehow, because you lived through that experience, many people, especially those who only barely know you, often seem to want to think your words have more weight. You lived through something they cannot imagine so they also cannot imagine that you didn't come out of the experience wiser. It is as if I'm Harry Potter or something. I'm "The

Dad Who Lived."

That's not me. I am not a hero, not even in my own mind (that's kinda sad, actually). Or at least I don't think that's me. Maybe I'm wise beyond even my ability to ascertain wisdom. Nah. That's why I brought in a pinch-hitter for this part.

Rev. Brent Powell is the director of Chaplain Services at St. Jude. He is an Episcopalian minister and he helps oversee the efforts of the four full time chaplains at his hospital. He also arranges services for patients and their families when they have religious needs outside the realm of what a hospital chaplain can handle. For example, if an Orthodox Jewish family came to St. Jude and needed specific services, Powell would be the person who reached out to the nearest Orthodox community to help make any needed arrangements.

The vast majority of hospitals will have someone in Rev. Powell's position. I've talked to several chaplains during David's many trips to the hospital and while working on this book. I've always found them to be very compassionate, caring, and comforting people regardless of their religion or denomination. It didn't seem to matter to them that I am not a member of their faith or their specific congregation.

It's amazing, really. They are there to help. If they can't help, they will do whatever it takes to find people who can. If nothing else, I've found that they can be great listeners, sounding boards for whatever you've got going on in your head.

Powell said the first few days after a diagnosis are fairly

similar for most people. The confusion, fear, and doubt seem to be universal. "The issues pretty much seem the same for the individual regardless of their religious affiliation," he said.

Some people who are particularly religious might find themselves having a crisis of faith right about now. Powell says that is fairly normal. I imagine that many of these people are those who ascribe to the idea that this is all part of God's plan (regardless of who/what that God is) and that they shouldn't question it, that whatever happens is what is supposed to happen. The crisis comes in, however, when these people begin to look for meaning.

"A normal part of the process is to question (why their child became ill)," Powell said. "They may internalize that questioning, or keep it inside. They might feel ashamed for questioning God."

Most metropolitan hospitals, especially those large enough to have a dedicated pediatric oncology unit, will have at least one full-time chaplain, maybe even a team. Most chaplains will have a Master's of Divinity degree and more than 1,600 hours of clinical training to learn how to work with people of all faiths. Many will even seek National Board Certification from the Association of Professional Chaplains. On top of that, they will usually have countless hours of day-in-day-out working with people and trying to help them while they are at their lowest points, looking for a way up.

The chaplains' job isn't necessarily to preach, especially when they are away from a pulpit. Powell said chaplains will often simply listen and provide a moral/ethical sounding board. They are there to help, not judge. People, regardless of their faith, will usually know how to follow their heart after they've had a chance to take a step back, talk, and think about their situation.

I'm sorry that I couldn't reach the priest from SLCH that performed David's baptism. He and I met casually in the chapel one afternoon and started talking. We spoke on and off during the months of David's treatment and he helped me work through my feelings. He wasn't judgmental and he never tried to push me. He just listened.

I'm sure he would have been willing to talk to me for this book but, as with David's nurses, I'm not sure I could have kept myself emotionally strong enough to get through that interview.

"It's not about what we say to people. It's about providing a format, a platform, a safe place where they can talk," Powell said. "It's someone who is willing to be there with you, to listen as a third party when you are in that state, that fog. When you are questioning and sleep deprived and have to make difficult (moral) decisions."

When a new patient comes into the hospital, they will likely be assigned a chaplain. This chaplain will probably conduct an informal assessment, similar to that conducted by a social worker. The chaplain looks at how the family views spiritual and/or religious matters and how they've dealt with any similar situations.

"We identify the coping strengths the family has and how the family sees the role of God in their situation," Powell explained, adding that the assessment could be as formal as a set of questions or as informal as a simple conversation. This assessment usually will include the entire family even, when appropriate, patients and their siblings. "We become a spiritual companion for them to walk with them through this process."

Dr. Soell said he sees faith come into play frequently during his therapy sessions and that people with a strong religious conviction have something in common.

"I believe people who have faith tend to have a greater support system. Greater, as in larger," he said. "Being part of a group, any group, helps as long as they are providing support."

Grief

Sooner or later, every parent with a seriously ill child faces grief. This is true regardless of whether the child lives or dies and regardless of what caused the illness or injury. Even if your child emerges alive and relatively unscathed you are going to face some levels of grief.

It just makes sense. Your life and the life of your child are going to change because of this situation. There is always a chance of relapse, rejection, or re-injury. Your child could end up in a wheelchair or you might just have second thoughts about allowing him or her to play sports. He or she might have a physical scar from surgery. Regardless of what the change is, you have to get used to seeing the world a little differently. You cannot help but grieve the loss of your old life and your old perspective. The world just doesn't seem as safe anymore.

"It is absolutely an evolutionary process," explained Dr. Soell. "There are lost dreams, especially with an infant. There is a hypothetical wonder about what our child is going to be. When doors close we feel more confined emotionally and we grieve that loss."

There is a song by Kenny Chesney, "Who You'd Be Today," that destroys me emotionally whenever it comes on the radio. Again, country music is my emotional bane. Ultimately the song seems to ask the question that we all wonder about after a loss even if the child survives. What kind of person would this child have been if they'd had the chance to grow up without this disease?

Dr. Soell told me a story about a teenaged patient of his who had recently learned that he had leukemia. This young man had the confidence of youth, especially when his oncologists gave him a very good prognosis. He didn't believe he was going to die. Instead, this young man grieved the fact that his cancer treatment would make him miss out on some of the high school experiences he'd been looking forward to. This grief, while not about a life coming to an end, was very real. One of the young man's dreams was dying.

"He was grieving the cancer, but he was also grieving that he couldn't play football. Throughout his treatment, there were multiple things to grieve (even though the young man wasn't dying). It is normal and healthy to grieve the multiple losses that take place."

In her book, *On Death and Dying*, Elizabeth Kubler-Ross identifies stages of grief that terminally ill patients go through (if they have time, that is). St. Louis Children's Hospital social workers Lennell Jackson and Kelly Olson both agree with Kubler-Ross and say parents of terminally or seriously ill children go through very similar stages. These stages are: Denial, Anger, Bargaining, Depression, and, finally, Acceptance.

In the Denial stage people tend to put off thinking about their problems. The issues are too big to deal with all at once so a small part of your rational mind takes a vacation and lets you think about other things for a while. Deep down you are aware. You know what's really going on, but you are spared some of the immediate shock. You don't want to admit to yourself that the situation is as serious as it is. It's normal. Nobody wants this. Wallowing in this stage, however, doesn't help.

Action Dad will either breeze through this stage because he is in a go-go-go place and he is always ready for the next step, or he will get stuck here for a while. He might not want to admit to himself that his go-go-go plans are about to take a detour. Cancer and other illnesses don't fit into his designs and that can be a hard thing for Action Dad to accept. By the same token, the Thinker Dad might get stuck here too because he's already thought out this child's entire life. Getting sick wasn't part of the plan. It's like the Spanish Inquisition. Nobody expects cancer (My apologies to Monty Python).

The Anger stage features tension, outbursts, resentment, bickering and other sorts of nasty behaviors that are unacceptable in most cases. Be careful, Action Dad. This can be an especially tough stage for you. Having a major problem, such as a serious injury or illness or even a recent or impending death, is not an excuse for lashing out at the people around you. However, most people are willing to accept your behaviors for a while if they know what's going on. Don't take too much advantage of this. Remember what you are really angry about. Screaming at your wife because she forgot to program the automatic coffee maker isn't going to cure cancer. Cancer is what you are really mad about.

In the Bargaining stage people start trying to find new ways around their problem. Often their prayers can include phrases like, "Please let me take his place," or "I'll do anything you want. I'll go to church regularly. I'll tithe. I'll quit swearing," etc.

Bargaining might look a bit different for people who are not religious. They might make extra efforts to get their lives in order. They might look for that regimented, orderly place outside of themselves that they've been missing – fixing problems in their lives without regard for some otherworldly deity. They might think, "If I make _____ right, then other parts of life will fall into line."

Unfortunately, bargaining only seems to work at the flea market. If you're inclined to indulge in the bargaining stage, make the best of it. Make your life better but realize that you can't talk cancer down to a lower price no matter how much you beg.

Depression is a stage that has more written about it than any other. I'm not going to tell you anything here that you don't already know. All I'll say is to watch out for yourself and know that it is okay to ask for help if you need it. Do not let this get out of hand. Pay attention to yourself. Pay attention to your spouse, your children, your family, and your friends. Watch for negative signs of serious depression in them and listen to them if they come to you warning you of the signs they've seen in you.

The last stage is Acceptance. I don't know if I'm actually there yet and David has been gone for a long time. This stage is where someone finally understands that a change has happened (or is about to happen), and there is nothing they can do about it. The only thing left is to come to terms with the change and begin picking up the pieces of your life. Here is where a positive attitude will be the biggest help.

"One day you sort of wake up and say, 'Life is good and I'm going to go on living,'" Jackson said. "The families that are the healthiest are the ones that recognize that this is behind us. They do what they have to do to keep themselves together. Whatever you need, you need to acknowledge it and accept it as normal. It takes whatever it takes."

A few years ago the Weber family started a new tradition. We launch balloons on David's birthday from the playground where there is a tree planted in his honor. I'm not gonna lie. It was tough the first few years. Now, it's something we look forward to. We gather friends who supported us during his illness and newer friends who have supported us since his passing. We say a few words then let helium balloons fly.

It used to be hard to do the launch when Maggie was younger. She didn't understand why we let the balloons go when it was so much more fun to hold on and play with them. She learned about her brother this year, so she is starting to understand why we do some of the things we do. Maybe this kind of thing helped bring me closer to the acceptance stage.

Jackson sees parents and families at all stages of the grief process every day. Surprisingly, she says the people she worries most about are not the ones who collapse, sobbing onto the floor. Instead, she is most concerned about the parents who seem to be living their everyday, normal lives without any emotional connections at all.

"The ones you worry about are the ones who don't deal with it

at all. They walk around like robots. They seem to be functioning and getting by, but they aren't," she said.

The warning signs that someone isn't handling their grief well are very similar to those of any other kind of clinical depression. People who are not dealing with their grief will tend to go to extremes. They will either eat too much or they will not eat enough. They will sleep all night and all day or they will be awake for days on end. Substance abuse is also common (I know I made some mistakes and handled my problems in that unhealthy way occasionally myself – Southern Comfort is not my friend) so watch out for people who are drinking too much alcohol, smoking too many cigarettes, or using too much of other controlled substances. Those kinds of escapes don't last and, if left unchecked, can end up doing way more harm than good.

An odd thing about the five stages of grief is that we don't have to go through them in order. Judith Hicks, a licensed clinical social worker at St. Jude, said it's okay to skip around a bit. In fact, we don't have to go through all five of the stages. It's possible to miss one entirely.

"Elizabeth Kubler-Ross never meant for us to take it like that, that you have to go through all of these stages in that order," she said, adding that she prefers to think of them as "symptoms" of grief instead of stages.

I've joked about how I was in denial about being in denial. I knew from the start that David's illness was serious and that there was a good chance that he could die. Sure, I was confident that the

chemotherapy and the liver transplant surgery would save him, but I don't think I was in denial about the gravity of the situation. Could this have been that I was refusing to reach the Acceptance stage about the Denial stage?

I'm not a doctor and, other than a couple of general psychology classes in college, I haven't had any training as a psychologist, but I think it may be easier for fathers to deal with the Anger stage, especially Action Dads like me. Maybe we mask the Depression stage as a prolonged version of the Anger stage. This could be because it is more culturally acceptable for men to be angry and less acceptable for them to be sad. Let's face it, nobody wanted to see Stallone's Rambo character in group therapy to deal with his unresolved issues about the Vietnam War. We wanted to see him blowing stuff up during *First Blood* and the subsequent sequels. We're OK with anger but not so much with weakness and/or vulnerability.

I'm sure the idea of a prolonged Anger stage was true in my case. I guess I was more comfortable being mad than I was being vulnerable. I found myself snapping at people more often. Friends and coworkers accepted my anger. They knew I was going through a problem. Crying, however, isn't as accepted. For many people crying is synonymous with weakness and being weak during a crisis isn't accepted.

During those first few weeks after David's initial diagnosis, I was mostly okay and although I was a bit more irritable than normal, I don't remember too many big blow ups. Rachel may tell a different

story, but I don't think I handled things too badly. Perhaps I was still in some state of persistent shock. I focused so much on being positive and staying active during those first few weeks that I don't think I had time for any other emotions. There were times when I'd drive to the grocery store three or four times in a night just so I could stay busy with something, anything, that I could call important. I was pushing myself and putting on a front. This might have been part of the denial stage. I'm not sure.

Then the diagnosis changed. We were told that the cancer had spread and that David had about a year to live. Yeah, I'm pretty sure that's when the Anger stage came out and all emotional bets were off. I'm not proud of this, but I know I vented quite a bit during those few weeks. I let loose on a lot of people and I'm sure many of them didn't deserve the treatment they received. However, I also found a new sense of courage and freedom to speak out during that time. I didn't hold back from unloading on people who deserved it. I said whatever I was thinking where before I might have held back. What could they possibly do to me that would be worse than what I was already going through?

One case I remember vividly occurred at school. I unleashed Hell on a coworker, giving voice to all the venom I possessed. The details are ugly and I can only defend my actions by saying that it was an incident that had been building for a while (even before David was diagnosed). Someone should have talked to her about her boorish behavior but, given my state of mind, it maybe shouldn't have been me.

This incident happened only a few moments before I got a call from Rachel telling me to get over to the hospital right away. David had been in for some routine tests. Maybe I was nervous. Maybe some kind of intuition told me that things weren't going to be good. The doctors reassessed their original prognosis. Instead of the better part of a year to live, they told us that David had about three weeks to live.

Unbelievably, that co-worker stopped by David's hospital room that night. Looking back, I have to admire the brass balls it took for her to walk into a lion's den like that. She knew I was furious and, more importantly, she knew that the fury had been directed at her. I kept myself together and held my temper in check as I met her at the hospital room door. I stood in front of the door, my body language showing that there was no way I was going to let her in the room, and said, "I'm sorry for the way I handled things today. I'm not sorry for what I said, but I am sorry for the way I said them. Thank you for coming by." Then I stepped back and quietly shut the door.

I've since been told that I became a hero to some other co-workers because of the way I handled that situation in telling off someone who desperately needed to be put in her place. In this instance the Anger stage worked for me, but most often it is counterproductive and I don't recommend languishing there too long. Like a lot of other things that are bad for you, anger can be habit forming. You don't need that right now.

Months after David died, I was still dealing with the Anger stage, but it had shifted a bit. I wasn't angry with God or lashing out at anyone undeservedly. I did maintain at least some of my verbal courage and didn't hold back as much as I previously had. Taylor Mali, one of my favorite modern poets has a line I like to use. He says he has a policy about honesty and ass-kicking. If you ask for either of them, he is obliged to give it to you.

In the months that followed David's death, I found myself feeling a lot of resentment and that wasn't like me. I'm not generally a resentful person, still at times I was really bothered by the happiness that other people felt, especially if those emotions were inspired by babies. What right did they have to be so damned happy and proud of their new baby or their pregnancy or their child's first day of kindergarten when I wouldn't get to have those things? The closer someone was to me the worse I felt and the more despicable my thoughts. I never wished to trade places with anyone, but I'm ashamed to admit that I came close.

Well, that was stupid of me. I couldn't help how I felt, but I recognized that life moved on. Ultimately, I had to ask myself some hard questions before I could accept happiness in other people. I had to recognize that some of these people were my dearest friends, and they had supported me through the darkest time in my life. I had to ask myself out loud if I thought they deserved to have their own lives and their own special moments.

Once I did that, it was obvious that I was being unreasonable. I had to accept that, if I really loved these people as much as I thought I did, then I would want them to be happy during all of those moments as deeply as they possibly could. Instead of being angry about the fact that they were still enjoying their families, I tried to take in a bit of the reflected happiness and feel joyful for them and with them. It sounds corny, but it helped and it made me more open to accepting my own happiness again.

I'm still dealing with the anger part. I still feel some resentment, but now it is mostly aimed at people who really do not appreciate the gifts they have. I get angry and resentful toward parents who abuse or neglect their children. Unfortunately, as a public school teacher I have plenty of opportunities to express this emotion.

I had a principal who probably saved my life when she stood in front of a door and wouldn't let me leave her office to go confront a parent who had hurt one of my students. It turned out that the dad in question was a very well-trained martial artist, a Golden Gloves competitor with clear anger management issues. He probably could have killed me. I'd have been right, but I'd have also been dead.

To a lesser extent I also resent those parents who don't try to make an effort to make mundane things into something special. I'm trying to turn that resentment into something positive. I've taken to bringing an extra dollar or two with me whenever I go to the mall. I'll buy a few carousel tokens and then just leave them on top of the machine. Perhaps someone that honestly doesn't have the money for the ride will see the tokens sitting there and take a few moments to enjoy being a family.

Maybe I should explain things a little bit. The whole carousel-thing is important to me. It isn't just the title of this book. Shortly after we got David's initial diagnosis, I was spending some time at our local shopping mall. I don't remember what I was there to get, but I do remember sitting down in the food court for a little bit of people-watching.

I started off just looking for anything interesting, maybe a couple having a loud argument, a college-kid with an odd facial piercing, anything to keep myself occupied for a few minutes while I had a soda and tried to relax. Before too long I started noticing dads and their kids.

The first was probably a dad and his college-aged son out picking up some new clothes for the new semester. Another father/son combo I noticed was a dad with several preteen boys. Clearly none of the boys wanted to be seen with their father but just as clearly, their dad wasn't going to let them run around the mall without him. The last pair I saw, the one that really got to me, was a father and a little boy, probably only a little more than a toddler, enjoying the carousel.

I guess I froze. I started wondering if I'd ever get to have any of those moments with David. Would I get to have all of those Dad-moments that other men seemed to take for granted? Would I get to play catch with him in the backyard? Would I get to teach him how to drive or shave? Would I get to shake his hand the day he left for college? At the time, we still had high hopes for a successful transplant. Still, I couldn't help being a bit morbid and wondering if we'd really have the time we thought we did. I decided that I'd put riding the carousel on the top of my Daddy's To Do list. By God, nothing was gonna keep me from getting that one item checked off.

Eventually, a few weeks or months later, David seemed healthy and happy enough that we took him directly from one of our hospital visits to the mall so we could ride. He was in a great mood. His grin was infectious, which is just about the only infectious thing a cancer-kid can handle. He felt good and he really seemed to enjoy the carousel even though he was technically a little bit too young to ride. He couldn't even hang on to the pole by himself. It didn't matter. We told the ride operator what was going on and she let us on. It was probably one of the best days of David's life.

It was the worst day of mine.

We had taken him directly from the hospital to the mall because that was the day the doctors told us that David's cancer had spread. A transplant wasn't an option anymore. The doctors told us that, at best, he had a year to live. His best day was my worst. It was all a matter of perspective.

I try to keep that day in mind. Maybe I'm pushing things a bit too much, but sometimes I'll even walk right up to strangers and offer the tokens to them. I'll usually say something like, "Hey, I had a few left over from the last time I was here with my son. Would you like to take the child for a ride?" I've almost never had someone refuse the tokens and I'll take that as a sign that I'm doing the right thing. They seem to know that when you get the chance to do something special with your child, you take it.

Giving away the tokens is one of the rituals I've created as a way to keep David alive in my memory and to give his short life some relevance. There are several other rituals, or traditions if you prefer that term, that Rachel and I use. Every year on David's birthday, we visit the tree that was planted in David's memory and release helium balloons with our friends and family. Sometimes the balloons have special messages written on them, but usually they are just a symbol of letting go of the grief while holding on to the love.

We also maintain a tradition of inviting all of our friends with young children over to our house the weekend before Halloween for a night of pumpkin carving, holiday movies, and lots of food. We started this tradition the year David died because we'd heard David's God-siblings were worried about us. They wanted to know if we were doing okay, so we thought we'd show them that we are ready to spend time with children again.

Hicks said this kind of ritual can be an important way to keep the child in your hearts while letting the pain escape. The traditions do not have to be grand gestures or long-time commitments. Things like visiting special places, reliving happy memories and even watching certain television shows at the holidays, are all significant ways to keep love alive even after a child is gone.

"We talk to parents about honoring the memory and finding ways to maintain the relationship (with the child). The old thing in grief was about letting go, but how do you let go of your child?" she said. "It is whatever fits. Some people take great comfort in going to the cemetery every day because that's where you feel close. Some people never go back. A ritual is whatever you do with regularity to have that connection. That's what's important."

Powell agrees, adding that the old saying that time heals all wounds isn't accurate.

"Time has nothing to do with it. It is about one's ability to re-engage in life," he said. "People look for ways to memorialize their child and give their child a continued presence in their life."

Many hospitals, especially those with dedicated pediatric oncology units or other specialized pediatric care facilities, host special Day of Remembrance ceremonies each year. Some do it around certain holidays while others plan it for times when they believe the weather will be more conducive to an outdoor event. I was hesitant to attend the event at SLCH the year after David died. I thought it would be too soon and too difficult. Eventually, I changed my mind and I went.

It wasn't easy. There were pictures and audio letters as part of a multimedia presentation. I saw some families for whom the grief was very fresh and others where the long-closed wounds were reopened. I held myself together fairly well until I saw David's picture and the letter I'd written. Once that happened, I was just as obnoxious as everybody else.

Still, even in the midst of that grief, I saw something I didn't expect. I saw smiles and hope shining on some of the faces. There were parents there who had gotten past the pain, or who were at least able to deal with it in public, and who were ready to begin living again.

"Those (events) help us keep connected to each other and to that child. It is a bittersweet weekend. There are tears but there is also laughter," Hicks said of the SLCH Day of Rememberance. "The most important thing, the huge value of coming back is being with the other parents, those who are further down the road. You can see (the next stops on your own journey) in them."

People will tell you that grief gets easier with time. That's true, but only about halfway. It is true that life gets better. Grief hasn't gone away, but it also isn't a day-to-day companion like it used to be. I still get hit with some serious emotional blows, but they tend to be things I can't see coming. I might hear a song on the radio (why do I listen to the country stations?!?) or I will see one of David's nurses at the mall. Those unexpected events still shock me. The days get easier but the moments, those little moments, are just as tough as they've ever been.

As parents, we never know what the future holds. Perfectly healthy children can still have accidents. You don't want to be sitting, stunned, in a hospital someday wishing you'd have taken the time to make ordinary things into something special.

I don't give a lot of parenting advice but I do tell people two things: First, laugh when you can, cry when you must, and never apologize for how you feel.

Second, always ride the carousel.

Addenda

Things to consider while making difficult decisions:

*What your child wants. Is he or she old enough to discuss this issue?

*Staff recommendations.

*The overall goal of treatment.

*Your feelings about what a good parent would do.

*Your religious faith or moral beliefs.

*How will your decision affect the rest of your family? Have you discussed it with them?

*Pursuing comfort when a cure is no longer an option.

*Avoiding treatment if your child is suffering and treatment is not likely to work.

Source: *Facing Difficult Times*, a resource book given to families at St. Jude Children's Research Hospital.

What to Bring

1. **Documentation**: Bring anything you think you might need beyond your insurance card. Notes from previous doctor/hospital visits, lists of medications, all necessary phone numbers and e-mail addresses, etc. Also, a pad of paper and a few pens for taking new notes or writing down questions.

2. **Money**: A bit of spending money is always a good idea, but you might want to think about bringing a roll of quarters ($10) along too. Many long-term facilities have in-house laundry for patients (and families) to use. Also, many hospitals have vending machines for snacks, toiletries, etc. similar to those in hotels.

3. **Neck massager and heating pad**s: You never know exactly where you are going to be sleeping if you stay with your child. Some hospitals have pull-out beds in patient rooms, but others might only have a few chairs.

4. **Something to occupy your time**: You will have a lot of down-time while your child is in the hospital. Having books, magazines, DVDs, video games, playing cards, etc. will help you pass the time. Be sure to include items for your child and their siblings.

5. **Chargers**: Your cell phone. Lap-top, e-reader, etc. will run out of a charge sooner or later. (Also, be sure to check with the hospital for the rules about using such

devices. Sometimes these things can interfere with medical monitoring devices in use at the hospital.

6. **Snacks**: The hospital will have a cafeteria and will likely also have a vending area, but what are the chances that the one special thing you really want at the end of a stressful day will be there waiting for you? If you must have that specific type of tea or chocolate it is a good idea to bring your own.

7. **Ear plugs/Eye masks**: Sleeping may be a problem if you are easily distracted or if you wake up easily. These items can make resting a bit easier.

8. **Comfortable clothes**: Bring things that are easy to take care of (no ironing necessary) and are comfortable to wear for long days. This should include a hat of some kind because bed-head and missed showers are common. You might want to include an extra pair of footwear, such as slippers, flip-flops, etc.

9. **Toiletries**: Razors, two-in-one shampoo & conditioner (it saves space), deodorant, combs/brushes, hair accessories (such as ponytail holders), toothbrushes/pastes, etc.

10. **Personal medications**: The hospital should have your child's prescriptions, but you will need to bring enough of your own medicines to last throughout the stay.

About the Author

Phil Weber is an award-winning journalist, having spent more than 10 years in newsrooms. He has covered crime and courts, city government, and education. His work has appeared in newspapers across the country with news agencies like Associated Press and Reuters. He has had several columns, articles, poems, and short stories published in scholarly journals and literary magazines.

In 2005 Phil decided to move away from the hectic journalism pace in favor of pursing his other passion – education. He currently works as a teacher in Champaign, Ilinois, where he lives with his wife, Rachel, his daughter, Maggie, and their new puppy, Mouse. Phil and Maggie are working on a series of holiday-themed stories for children. She comes up with the ideas and he takes the credit by typing the stories into the computer.

Phil is available for speaking engagements to your group and for any media outlet that needs a motivated and engaging guest. Please contact him at alwaysridethecarousel.com for details.

On a related note, he is very self-conscious when it comes to writing about himself in the third-person. It feels awkward and unnatural to him.